# LIVING WITH BEREAVEMENT

---

Alex James

---

**RIGHT WAY**

Typeset in 11½ pt Times by Letterpart Ltd., Reigate, Surrey.

Printed and bound in Great Britain by Cox & Wyman Ltd., Reading, Berkshire.

The *Right Way* series is published by Elliot Right Way Books, Brighton Road, Lower Kingswood, Tadworth, Surrey, KT20 6TD, U.K. For information about our company and the other books we publish, visit our web site at www.right-way.co.uk

# DEDICATION

Steven Lissaman

5 June 1957 – 2 February 1970

My Childhood Friend

# ACKNOWLEDGEMENTS

All details of experiences within this book have been changed in order to protect the identity of the individuals. I wish to acknowledge everyone that I been privileged to meet and work with who have enabled me a deeper understanding of bereavement.

I would also like to express my gratitude to the following people who have been a continual source of inspiration to me throughout my personal and professional development:

*Lillian Beattie, Maggie Garside, Paula Kavanagh, Marilyn Fairclough, Sue George, Simon Jenkins, Jo Wyant – Mom to Jeremy (GPA), Mary Wilkinson.*

*Carlita Adams* – for her friendship, support and editorial skills during the writing of this book.

*My friend, Carol* – for her encouragement and unfailing belief in my ability.

*My family* – for their generous support and love.

# CONTENTS

# INTRODUCTION

Human beings, regardless of cultural, religious or historical backgrounds, are united by one common bond: the need to communicate and to know that they are not alone. The recognition that something they experience has also been experienced by another is both reassuring and a huge relief.

I spend much of my time confirming to those who grieve that they are not losing their minds and that the thoughts and feelings they are experiencing in grief are usual. (I hesitate to use the word 'normal', as everyone sets their own criteria as to the true meaning of that word.) There are large, unspoken and unexplored areas of death and of communication, even in today's technical, forward-thinking, fly-on-the-wall society, and I hope by reading this book you will find a deeper understanding and a greater ability to communicate with the bereaved.

Many bereaved people use imagery or metaphors to describe their feelings as they can feel that this is the only way they can communicate the true depth of their grief and loss to us. Sometimes, particularly where deep emotions are involved, commonly used words are not enough. When I heard a lady describe her grief as a 'bubble', I was aware of her sense of relief that she had finally found an image that exactly described her feelings. We don't want to be misunderstood; we work hard at enabling those that we wish to communicate with to understand.

Many grieving individuals don't talk about how they really feel; there are too many things left unsaid and thoughts that are not shared. The bereaved feel an unspoken pressure to conform and to avoid being seen as a nuisance. Their most overwhelming fear is that those in authoritative roles may label them as unstable.

I hope to change attitudes towards grief and towards the bereaved, and to support and activate work that improves all areas of communication, and so avoid causing further anxieties and distress to both the bereaved and their helpers and supporters.

# 1

# MESSENGERS AND HELPERS

Someone once described the experience of bereavement like this:

*"Once I had a puzzle, a jigsaw puzzle, a picture complete. I knew its pieces – how they fitted with me. I knew its shape and colour and I planned its future and size. Suddenly it's as though someone has taken everything I know and shaken it, thrown it up into the air and now I'm left with pieces – some of them are familiar but they no longer fit as they did, part is missing and it can never be the same."*

This use of language clearly describes this person's sense of disconnection. It wasn't enough to say, *"I feel lost"* or *"I can't put my life back"*; the image instantly and vividly conveys the sense of isolation and loss.

Death does change everything, and we cannot fix it or prevent it, but we can learn how to communicate with those who find themselves in that place where their life changes because of death. There are those who say that you cannot know or understand any experience unless you too have been through it. I disagree.

We are all individuals, and our experiences of life and death are as individual and unique as we are. How we manage any situation will not only depend on our current emotional capacity, but on other aspects and influences at that time. It is impossible for any one person truly to know how another feels. Understanding of others comes not from your own experience but from the ability to be with them and to hear and empathise, to take all that they have to say and to accept their words as they are, avoiding the urge to interpret them by your own measure or judgment. The stages of grief have been written and spoken about many times, but I wonder how useful it is to refer to grief as though there is a plan or mapped route to follow to guide you through these stages. Often people are confused or feel that they aren't 'doing it' right, the stages being interpreted by them as being set tasks that must be carried out in order to move forward. I spend much of my time confirming that they *are* 'doing it' properly and that there is only one way – their way. Each person's passage through grief is unique, but contained within it are threads that can be connected to the experiences of others. Our use of language, what we say, how we talk and, more importantly, how we listen, are the foundation of real communication. This first chapter is written for people who, either by the nature of their work or, through circumstance, find themselves communicating with the bereaved.

The messengers who deliver the news of a death to a family have a traumatic job indeed and, whilst acknowledging their feelings and anxieties, this chapter is about understanding how it feels to be the person receiving that news.

*"I was doing my ironing, I saw the police car pull up outside and I thought . . . oh, someone's in trouble. It didn't cross my mind that it could be me . . . not even when he came up the path and knocked at the door. I thought it must be for next door, he had a strange look on his face . . . I don't really remember all he said, just that he was sorry and that my husband had been killed in an accident at work. I thought he was joking. I thought he had got the wrong house. The lady police officer with him told me to sit down . . . I felt like things were very confused, muddled, I felt like I was disconnected . . . in a bubble . . . I wasn't in the right life suddenly. I know that sounds strange. I remember thinking that they were wrong and my body felt totally numb. I think I made the tea. We chatted but I can't remember what about except that the policeman seemed so young and I did say I was sorry that he had such an awful job."*

People are going about their everyday business and are unaware of the shattering news that they are about to receive. On receipt of the news, the shock may be so great that it is almost unacceptable. They may continue to do whatever they were doing at that time. The providers of the news may find the recipient offering them comfort. The recipient of the news is aware, on one level, of what is being said, but on another is so shocked as to be incapable of taking in the information. This can give the messenger/helper a false impression that, although shocked, the recipient is accepting and able to understand.

> *"After the police went I couldn't remember
> everything they'd said and I felt anxious panic that
> I had to do things, but might not remember
> everything. I couldn't recall things and it still felt so
> unreal . . . like – I'm talking to you now, but I'm
> distant behind glass."*

The use of language, the awareness of reaction and the ability to hear what is not being said is the key to communication. Speaking slowly, without effect or drama and using the simplest, shortest phrases and language, only adding details as the family request it are the other ways that those involved in the giving of information can be of huge assistance.

Once the family members are alone together, they will revisit being told and may not be able to recall details that have been given. They may appear to be extremely organised, seeking to gain control over an uncontrollable experience. They may seem efficient, lucid and, in some instances, supportive to others. They may continue with their work or whatever they were doing at the time. A police officer told me:

> *"I arrived at the house. The mother was mowing the
> grass. I told her about her daughter's death. After a
> short time she said that, before she could do
> anything else, she would have to put her lawn
> mower away or her husband would go mad if he
> came home and saw that she had left it out."*

The enormity of the news, the shocking revelation and its unreality create a protective bubble around the bereaved, a bubble that separates them from reality and acceptance.

It should never be assumed that reaction will occur in a certain way or can be interpreted as anything other than a variation of shock. In some instances, there may be euphoria, a kind of excited need to tell others.

*"After the police had gone I phoned my brother. I just said I hope you are sitting down Joe . . . Then I kind of blurted it out excitedly . . . John's dead. Afterwards I regretted telling him, because I suddenly thought, 'What if it's not true?' Then I hated that policeman and I began to feel mad as hell with my husband."*

There may be anger with the messenger, or at the deceased, or there may be guilt. The bringer of this news may appear to be at the calm centre of the trauma, while the shocked bereaved struggle with accepting and taking in all that they have been told.

*"I heard what the police officer said, but I felt he was talking about someone else. I began to feel a sense of unreality, of being disconnected, like I was in this bubble, seeing everything, hearing it, but not part of it. I phoned my children's school and told them, I arranged for them to be collected – I think the police offered but my neighbour went. I phoned my sister. I remember I was supportive to her shock but I felt disconnected from my own. After the police went I couldn't remember what or all they had said. The person I wanted most to talk to, to help me – my husband – wasn't there."*

The descriptions of being behind glass or in a bubble are, in my experience, the most commonly used descriptions.

The confirmation that others too feel this way enables and relieves the sense of isolation.

Sometimes professionals and family members may feel protective, it can be tempting to withhold information in the belief that it could be more damaging.

> *"I wanted to see my son, but the police officer said I shouldn't. He was my son; I wanted to know how he had died. I needed to hold him, to be with him but the funeral director said it might be better not to. I felt excluded . . . like I had deserted my son."*

When I asked why he felt unable to insist, he replied, *"I didn't want to be a nuisance."*

There seems to be a feeling that, once a loved one dies, the body becomes the property of the hospital or funeral director. In cases of death where there are suspicious circumstances or where there may be an autopsy, the body will not be released to the family and remains in the possession of the coroner. These are not the occurrences that I refer to when I say that it is not unusual for the bereaved to feel that their loved one has been taken from them in an unspoken way. They feel unable to touch or hold or ask questions. One lady told me that her husband was wrapped up in a sheet at the hospital with only his face visible. She felt unable to touch him. She said it felt too clinical and that she was aware that, if she disturbed that sheet, they would know she had done so and might not like it.

We can, as individuals, only reach our own conclusions by drawing on our own experiences. What one person may find sickening or unbearable, another may not. Protecting the bereaved from details that we find too difficult to stomach or distressing may hinder them from acceptance. In some cases it may send them along the road of potentially damaging fantasies which could, at a later stage, cause them regrets for allowing themselves to be pressurised into agreeing to decisions that others deemed best for them. It is of vital importance that some thought be given at this stage to the 'real' reasons for withholding information and that any fears of what may result if information is revealed are explored. It can be tempting to rescue, to cover up details and avoid facing the extra distress that their revelation may cause.

This is how I visualise grief and how I work with it to achieve real communication. The bereaved are in a deep, dark pit and reaching them can seem impossible. The immediate urge is to rescue; to throw in a ladder and compel them to climb out into daylight; to tell them that things are better once they get out and to recall stories of others who have survived.

How hard we work at rescue, but why? Because we think it is all we can do? The recognition of death is painful and our knowledge of death's impact, on all aspects of the lives of the people who are left, makes us want to be the one who helps them survive.

I climb down into that pit; I hear their story; I accept their words, thoughts and feelings, the bizarre and the frightening parts that they fear to share, their fears of being misunderstood or thought crazy. This is where they need to be. Resisting the temptation to rescue is hard and, for some, that temptation is too great. There is a deep need to care for the emotionally devastated, to tuck them up and make them safe, to protect them from reality, to offer hugs and hush their anguished words and stem their flow of tears. This care can cause the bereaved to become the pleaser, to deceive, hide their inmost thoughts and feelings, thus isolating themselves. To the outside world they appear to be 'doing well'. Oh, how we use that phrase around the bereaved. The 'doing well' blanket, the blanket of pressure that we wrap them in so tightly that we suffocate their deepest feelings.

These are the scary feelings, the thoughts and memories that often lie hidden whilst in the company of caring family or friends, but which in isolation, in the lonely hours, are taken out and examined and lived through. It's rather like sitting on the lid of an over-full box: eventually, it becomes so full that the contents cannot be contained and spill out uncontrollably.

> *"They ask how I am. I want to say, 'This is indescribable. I feel like someone's ripped my insides out. I feel so raw it's a real pain, a stabbing in my chest, in my heart. I feel like I have been skinned alive. I feel like I just want to die.' But I hold the lump in my throat, I force back the tears and I reply, 'Oh, you know . . . I'm doing OK.' They say, 'Great,'. . . they say, 'Time heals,'. . . They are relieved."*

We ask, "How are you?", and secretly hope that you'll say "Fine". It is rare to ask anyone at any time, "How are you?", and get the response, "Well, actually I feel like total shit!"

There are, it seems, unspoken rules to our communications which revolve around the acceptable response. It is acceptable to say, "I'm fine", but too scary to tell the real truth if it is anything other than "Fine".

> *"I wanted to see my wife. My brother said I shouldn't . . . I didn't want to upset him so I went*

*alone. The funeral director tried to say he thought I shouldn't. I felt angry that I had to find strength to argue my case so, in the end, I promised not to lift the small cloth over my wife's face. The funeral director came into the room with me. He kept spraying this aerosol. I knew it was to mask the smell; my wife couldn't be embalmed. The funeral director didn't speak. I felt like we were tainted. I felt like a child. Like I couldn't be trusted. I felt like he was watching me. I felt I couldn't say my goodbye."*

This is a clear example of non-communication: the bereaved person feeling afraid to ask, to have a need explained or a wish fulfilled. This 'withholding' or non-communication is common. People tell me that they often feel they must hide or excuse their sorrow and their needs, and appear coherent and managing or even apologetic.

They may fear that those who are professional or informed may judge them, find their questions tiresome or, in some way, strange. Too much is left unsaid. How can we change this? By changing our reaction to the bereaved, communicating with them; listening to their words and to what they are saying, not placing our interpretations on those words. We need to inform the bereaved of the facts in simple language that can be easily absorbed and allow space for them. We have to encourage them to absorb and manage as much as they feel able to at that time and support them in a non-intrusive way.

In making these changes, you are not attempting rescue but giving something far more beneficial and crucial to the process: Acceptance and Holding. This is demanding both physically and emotionally, but if yours is a mission to assist then you must refrain from rescuing, covering up or hushing their words.

There is also a need for balance. There are time-limits and official procedures that need to be addressed and maintained. If you can achieve the balance between these things, then the sense of holding will be increased and the bereaved will not feel that all control is gone from their life.

Whilst helping in a secondary school with bereaved teenagers, I observed that teachers were hesitant to give the bereaved youngsters homework or to ask them to complete tasks as 'they were grieving'. The teenagers did need time to grieve, but they also needed security and the confirmation that tasks have to be completed, and that life does continue. In the same way, grieving adults must be encouraged to make decisions and choices and allowed to undertake and complete tasks. When someone dies, the world does change and we feel out of control, leading to a sense of powerlessness and insecurity. All that we knew, and had thought would be forever, has gone. It is of vital importance that the ability to plan and make decisions is, if only in some small way, restored.

After the initial news of a death, the household may become very active, with visits by those involved, official paperwork to attend to, and funeral arrangements to make. All this happens at a time when the minds of the bereaved are in shock and in a dreamlike unreality. They may feel enclosed within the bubble of grief and on automated function. You may feel the need to assume responsibility for the arrangements that have to be made. However, whilst it may be necessary to assist with some practical tasks, the most crucial and beneficial assistance is simply to be there, to listen and allow the bereaved to talk repetitively about their feelings and experience, and to encourage their involvement with decisions or arrangements.

There can be feelings of a need to organise things quickly. It is frequently said or thought that, once the funeral is over, everyone will feel better and life will return to normality, but it should not be forgotten by the helper that this is the last opportunity for the bereaved to say goodbye to their loved one. Nothing should be done quickly. Time should be taken to talk and discuss with them how they would like their farewell to be, and assisting them as far as possible with arrangements. The bereaved often tell me that they can't remember the funeral, as they were numb and unable to take in all that was happening, and they feel cheated that such an important day passed in a blur and is lost. There may be frustration or anger with those who helped with arrangements, or towards those professionally involved.

*"I didn't think much at the time, I was disconnected, I feel I let him down; I left him to the care of someone he didn't know. I am worried that they didn't know him; he was a very private man. I feel intruded upon. I wish I had been there to see to him myself."*

A sense of deserting the loved one can be present. When I enquire why they didn't ask the funeral director whether they could be there and participate in the preparation, I am often told that they wanted to but felt scared that the funeral director might think they were weird, morbid or crazy.

There may be concerns about the state of the body

because of injury or decomposition but it should not be forgotten that this is the loved one of the bereaved. They do not see what we, who are more detached, may see. Neither is it unusual for the bereaved to say initially that they don't want to see the deceased, and then to change their minds but feel that they cannot ask later.

*"I left him at the hospital. I wish I'd brought him home; I wish I'd had time with him . . . I didn't want to be a nuisance."*

The need to give ongoing care to the deceased is very real, yet the unspoken taboos and secrecy that still exist around funeral parlours prevent this and keep out the bereaved. Years ago, when someone died, the body was often brought home and laid out by the family. In some cultures today preparation of the body is undertaken by family members and this, in my experience and opinion, can be beneficial to the bereaved, as it enables them physically to embrace their loved one's death and to extend their care to the body. It is not unusual to want to take photographs, or a lock of hair, or to feel the need to hold on to every last part before the final goodbye. Many people say that they longed to take a photo, but felt that this may be refused them. How is it that, as a society, we find it acceptable to watch on television the funerals of the famous, yet find the videoing of the funeral of our loved ones still taboo? People often wish that they had videoed the funeral so they could watch it at a later date and feel part of it, as, at the time, they couldn't remember very much.

Gentle reassurance is needed. Whatever they want is all right and there are no do's or don'ts, because the experience of death is as unique as those experiencing its impact. How it is managed by each person will depend on that individual's emotional, physical and psychological background and life experience.

I wrote earlier of the sense of shocked unreality, and how it may prevent the bereaved from taking in information, although they may appear to be listening. Writing everything down using simple terms and clear instructions can be of huge assistance; as can leaving a list of telephone numbers by the telephone so they are easily accessible and perhaps a list of items that need to be organized, also showing which items are already being attended to, and by whom.

It is important where possible to offer choices, although the response may be one of indecision. Allow the bereaved space and time. Try to avoid the temptation to succumb to your own feelings of wanting to protect or spare them added trauma. It is fundamentally important, in this intimate involvement with the newly bereaved, to lay one's own self aside, to be non-judgmental and to offer regard and respect for their wishes; to be part of their journey through grief, not the driving force.

### Panic Attacks, Anxiety and Phobias

Anxiety is often apparent in the early days and can manifest itself in many ways. Fear of going out is not unusual, or an overwhelming sense of panic once outside. They may have the desire to get away, so it is useful to talk through and to plan any outings. Discuss where and when they are going, how they intend to get there, what could happen if they meet people they know and, if this happens, how they wish to manage it. I call this preparation 'safety netting': putting in place something that gives a sense of security and reassurance at a time when everything may feel unsafe and insecure. You cannot change what has happened, but you can assist the bereaved to manage by trying to pre-empt potential emotional situations. It is also important that pressure is not put upon the bereaved to continue with a task that adds anxiety.

> *"I had been to order the flowers . . . it seemed so unreal. I needed to get some shopping too and I was OK at first but then I felt this rush of fear. I felt like I had to run, to get out of the shop, to get home . . . it was really scary."*

Often anxieties are unexpected, or may seem bizarre and therefore left unspoken, so leaving the bereaved to struggle with their feelings in isolation.

> *"I had been fine on the morning of the funeral . . . I had this sense of peace, of calm. I was able to think. I even managed to talk to a neighbour and I felt in touch after the last few days where I had felt so disconnected. Then it happened. We were in the car behind the hearse and I began to panic. I wanted to get out. I felt stifled like I couldn't breathe. I just wanted to get away. I kept my face turned towards the window and felt every bone in my body tense, I thought I would snap . . . it was like being trapped."*

The sense of being trapped is a real feeling to the bereaved as there is no escape from the situation and the feelings of needing to get away from it are often frighteningly intense. Someone else described his anxiety of being afraid that other people would think he didn't care as he couldn't cry. He tried but felt totally numb, empty and all cried out.

> *"I felt anxious and angry with myself, a fraud, that they were all watching me and I wanted to cry but I couldn't. I was sitting in the chapel thinking I don't look like a mourner; if I don't cry they will think I'm OK. They'll think I didn't care."*

The fear of being out of control and on display are also sources of anxiety.

> *"I had planned all that I wanted to say, but, as I tried to speak, it wouldn't happen. I felt overwhelmed. I couldn't stop sobbing. I felt exposed and on show – and like I had let her down."*

These very different experiences share a similar pattern: the expectation to behave or react in a certain way and the feelings of being observed and of exposure. In grief there is vulnerability. The usual protective guards that we have in place to help us mask those feelings we wish to control or to manage are no longer accessible. The sensations of vulnerability and fragility can be all-consuming. The day of the funeral often passes in a haze of making conversation but not participating in the ritual.

> *"It feels like I am watching a film. I know I am there but I don't feel part of it."*

The bereaved may find they are supporting others who cling tearfully to them exhibiting their grief and requiring the bereaved to comfort them. If 'safety netting' can be put in place prior to the funeral, the bereaved will know that at a later time they will have some time and space to themselves.

After the funeral, the sense of loss and reality can suddenly overwhelm the bereaved, who may need to talk through the day of the funeral and revisit events that have happened over the past few days. It is usual for them to be repetitive, necessary for them to feel heard. This can cause anxiety for the listener who may not know what to say or how to respond. This too is normal. By listening and accepting, you are helping the bereaved to work through their experience, so they can start to make some sense of it and accept the reality. It is also helpful if you tell them that you do not know what to say, as this comment is often received with relief by the bereaved person. Many bereaved people have told me that, after the funeral, they had thoughts and feelings that they wanted to share. But they felt unable to speak of them, for fear of what others might think. They often have concerns about the body of the deceased (if it has been buried) and especially about its safety.

> *"I couldn't bear it . . . I hadn't expected to feel like that at the graveside. Someone gave me some dirt to throw . . . I couldn't throw dirt on my baby. It felt brutal, I wanted them to stop, I wanted to lift him out and take him home."*

This feeling of wanting to care for and bring the body home is very common and when this is confirmed as being quite usual there is relief.

A grieving mother told me that she just couldn't tell anyone, not even her husband that she had, for some time, felt a strong desire to dig up their dead child. It was very difficult for her as she knew that she couldn't do it but, at the same time, she longed to hold onto and care for the remains of her child. The thought of the cold and the wet and the decomposition of the body troubled her, but she felt unable to share these fears and desires. We discussed these feelings and afterwards she went home and told her husband, who broke down and told her that he too had felt that way and it was a huge relief to him to know that she shared these thoughts.

Well-meaning family and friends can unwittingly exert pressure on the bereaved person to pack up the belongings of the deceased immediately after the funeral. There is no time-limit on when or how these tasks are done. Reassurance that nothing has to be done at speed, and that they can be done in their time and at their own pace, is often much needed. The bereaved may gain comfort by wearing the clothes of their loved one, by carrying them around or sleeping with them. Their sense of loss can increase when the smell of their loved one begins to fade from these precious items of clothing or from the room. Changing the bedding where the deceased slept can be unbearably hard. A mother told me that she couldn't move or change anything in her child's room after he had died and often got into his bed where she felt a closeness and comfort in the smell of her child. A husband told me he couldn't bear to sleep in the bed that he had shared with his wife. It was too painful. These differences in people's reactions confirm the diversity of grief. These behaviours can seem bizarre or be distressing to people who are less involved, but confirmation that they are usual and acceptable may be all that the bereaved person needs to help them through that immediate period of time.

I say for 'the immediate period', as boundaries and limitations are important and cannot be under-estimated. It is vital to the healing process that the bereaved retain the sense of security and acknowledgment that life does continue after a death. Their getting back to life can in itself create vast areas of emotion, guilt, anger and vulnerability.

*"About a week after the funeral I decided to go back to work. I got ready that morning, it was incredibly hard, I had to make myself get up and dress. Just as I was leaving the house I saw a neighbour, she waved, it seemed normal, too normal.*

*I waved back, she approached, I began to feel anxious and then she said to me, 'I'm glad to see you getting back to normal.'*

*Normal – normal can never exist again for me. I felt guilty, like she thought I was over it, like it must seem to everyone that I'm over it. I wanted to scream out, 'It's not normal, my daughter is dead.' I needed to go to work but I felt like I was deserting my grief, I felt vulnerable and exposed. Everyone in the street knows she's dead. What were they thinking?"*

The action of returning to work is extremely hard; there can be unexpected triggers. The workplace itself can be a trigger: *"The last time I sat in that chair he/she was alive."*

A teenager, whose mother died suddenly, told me he felt guilty for being the centre of attention and for liking the attention. At the same time he didn't want to share his feelings, as he was frightened he would not be able to recover them if he let them out, and that would make him vulnerable.

The diversity of feelings within grief is enormous and confusing for the bereaved. The fear of letting go, of becoming uncontrollably distressed and overwhelmed by emotion and of being unable to recover the person he or she used to be. There are also feelings of anxiety about being asked, and anger with those who do not ask, the frustration that no-one is asking or seeming concerned about their feelings, that people are uninterested. Managing a return to life after bereavement is physically and emotionally draining and that coupled with a deep grief leave the bereaved mentally exhausted. Simple tasks may become increasingly harder and physical symptoms may be apparent, such as loss of appetite, the inability to concentrate and disinterest in the world in general.

As the weeks pass, the bereaved become more aware of the enormity of their loss. As the cushion of shock slips away they are left with reality and, eventually, acceptance. The pressure to be 'doing well' or 'getting over it' increases and opportunities to talk about their loved one decrease. A sense of isolation manifests itself around them.

Other events may cause additional trauma, such as attendance at an inquest. The experience of revisiting the day of the death and of hearing the story again, without preparation or professional support, may transport the bereaved back in time without the protective bubble of numbness. They are exposed to the reality of their loved one's death. Unexpected information and revelations known only to the family could be aired in public and disclosed to the press, causing added trauma, anger, frustration and grief. Some coroners are aware of these aspects and know how language can be tailored so as to be sensitive to the grieving family. Unfortunately not all police officers, coroners, medical staff or coroner's assistants are aware and sensitive to these issues and can unwittingly be the cause of added anguish. It is advisable for the bereaved to be prepared for attendance at inquests and there are agencies that offer this support.

Celebrations, e.g. Christmas, family gatherings and anniversaries of the death, are times when the bereaved may feel extremely anxious and the importance of talking through, pre-planning and 'safety netting' cannot be over-emphasised. The bereaved are often not consulted on the way that they want to spend these occasions; they are cajoled and almost bullied into participating. Little consideration may be given to whether they actually want to be part of a crowd. The need to 'jolly' them out of grief and to force them to get their lives back to 'normal' could be more to do with other people's sense of security and their need to get things back to how they feel it should be. This is, of course, impossible as life has been changed by loss and will never be the same again. People are changed by death, and it is only by accepting that this change is permanent that grief becomes a little more manageable.

There is a need for everyone to be educated about death and about its impact on individuals, not only from a medical or textbook psychological or analytical stance but also from a personal and humane angle. It is not enough to offer condolences or a listening ear. It is not enough to accept the standard phrase "I'm doing OK" because it relieves us from finding the 'right' words and facing up to our own inadequacy, clumsiness and embarrassment.

Sometimes words are not enough. I have talked about the relief of the bereaved in knowing that they are not unique in their experience. Through my work I often connect to people by using the experience and the language of another grief-stricken person to create a common ground between those who grieve.

Those I work with often accept the description of life as a puzzle and its missing pieces. "That's it . . . That's how I feel."

A father, whose teenage child died suddenly, told me:

*"I felt like I'd got some clay, I made this vase, it took ages moulding it and it was almost ready to fire, to be something I could look at and see finished, but then it was dropped. Smashed and gone."*

By using these visual illustrations the bereaved are able to communicate with me and to describe a small part of how they feel. We may be lost for words and worried that anything we say or do would be inadequate or insufficient. But there is, I believe, in all of us, the ability to communicate with a person at the time of greatest emotional need, and to find the necessary words and phrases to enable him or her to move through grief towards acceptance.

# 2

# DEATH OF A PARENT

Most of us hope that we will live a long and healthy life, and, when we are too old to care, we will die peacefully and gently in our sleep. We accept, because we have to, that with age our bodies deteriorate and that we may become infirm and unable to do the things we used to. If we are well, mentally alert and have lived a moderately healthy lifestyle we may expect to achieve a 'ripe old age' which I think of as somewhere around my mid to late nineties.

As we grow older we push what we feel is 'old' further from ourselves. Life is a process and in the expected order of life we accept that our elderly relatives, grandparents and then parents will die leaving us behind. If our parents are elderly, losing the senses and faculties that give quality to their lives, or if we have had to nurse or be involved in the care of an elderly parent there may be a sense of relief when life ends. For many though, the relief may go hand in hand with a deep sense of sudden loneliness. These feelings are rarely shared because when one's parents are elderly and one is middle aged and perhaps a parent oneself society gives little regard to the loss. It is expected, the norm and order of life.

Whilst our parents are alive we are still the children of that relationship. When they die, no matter what our age, we are orphaned. Even though throughout our lives there is the unspoken acceptance that one day our parents will die, it seems far away in the distance and something that will happen in the future.

A 60-year-old man whose parents had recently died said:

> *"I am an orphan now, I feel alone, my roots are gone – maybe I am next, I am moved up a notch, I am the old one in the family now.*
> *It isn't that they are gone so much but that I am left behind. The world is changing too quickly and my most stable and familiar are gone. I am relieved for them; my mother was sickly for years and feared dying painfully – it was a blessing that she slipped away gently in her sleep."*

The deep loss felt by this gentleman after the death of his parents is not at all unusual, or unique, but is rarely talked about. We somehow expect a person who has a family of his own and whose parents are in their late eighties to relinquish being the child and to let go with ease.

I remember the funeral of my father-in-law's mother. We, the younger generation all being in our twenties and thirties, gathered together afterwards in the same social way that we might at a wedding or other family social event. Some spoke of Nana's great age, she was 93, others recalled memories of her living in a certain house where they had visited but of this group the thought seemed to be that as Nana had lived a long life it was acceptable that she had died. My husband's parents and their siblings also grouped together, chatting and reminiscing; there were a few tears but there was, it seemed, an acceptance. This was the expected order and her longevity seemed to make her death easier to bear.

On the other hand, perhaps the expectation may have created an unspoken pressure for the older children, my husband's parents, to sit on their grief. How would it affect the younger generations if the children of the elderly deceased were to express their loss, their grief, their fear and their sense of being left parentless? What could we offer? Our expectation is that perhaps with age comes acceptance of a parent's death.

During the last century the two World Wars brought with them a tragic loss of young life. Perhaps in those bygone days there was no time to indulge in grief. With so much loss and a need to survive, the focus became getting on with life, moving on. This attitude towards death and loss would have affected our parents and grandparents; they may have grown up being expected to show a 'stiff upper lip' and exhibit 'backbone', and perhaps these ways of thinking have influenced our present day behaviour towards bereavement. We feel pressured to be 'doing well' and to say "I'm OK". We feel awkward asking questions and, not knowing what to say, we find it easier to say nothing at all.

We are changing and becoming more aware of feelings. The 'big boys don't cry' and 'stiff upper lip' attitudes of the past are finally being seen as less acceptable and no longer the expected emotions.

For some, though, especially the older generations, the control of their emotions is something that can be used as a method of retreat from the outside world. They may have been brought up in a more controlled world than the younger generations and some can feel it is shameful to exhibit their grief in public or to wear their hearts on their sleeves. Younger people, who have been brought up in a more 'touchy-feely' world, can find this difficult to understand, but, for some, grief is a private matter not to be shared with anyone except intimate and close family or friends. Some elderly bereaved people may respond to a genuine enquiry about their well being with an "I'm fine". This does not mean that they do not appreciate being asked or that they mourn their loss any the less than a person who is more open about their feelings.

Whilst our mother or father is alive, no matter what their age, we have an anchor, a tangible link to our childhood. Their presence on the earth confirms that we are not only parents, middle-aged or perhaps grand-parents, but that we are still someone's child.

*"I wish people, friends, family even, could understand how I feel. My Dad died young – well in his 60s – but Mum lived on to her 90s. When my Dad died I was 38, people were more supportive, they were interested in how I was. There were some who, when they learned his age, 62, said, 'Oh well, he was getting on', like it was OK. I wasn't ready for his death, I still needed him there. Now my Mum has died, I just feel so lost. She was senile but she was there. I could go to visit her and somehow her being there gave me a sense of security. This sounds silly. I mean I'm almost 70, but no-one seems to be interested – even my children.*

*It's like it doesn't matter because Mummy had a 'good innings' as they say and that makes it acceptable. It's like I'm suddenly faced with my own age, my own mortality and it does feel just as painful as when my Dad died."*

For many children as their parent's age, deterioration, illness or inability set in there is often a dilemma of 'What to do about Mum or Dad?' If there are siblings this may be discussed and the care shared. Some parents make arrangements for themselves and take time to plan for their future, for possible care that may be needed. However, with the spiralling costs of care homes and the closures of many council-run care homes in the UK, children may be faced with caring for an elderly parent themselves. This can be an exhausting task, a task of commitment and can be the cause of resentments not only for the carer but for other family members who may have to adjust their lifestyles in order to facilitate an elderly relative.

*"I promised my father that I would always care for my mother. He died of cancer at the age of 70. My mother lived alone until she was in her mid-eighties, but, after a fall, I felt that she needed more constant on-hand care. My children were at university and we, my husband and I, decided to convert a downstairs room for her. I never knew how much it was going to impact my family. At first it was manageable, Mother could do some things alone, but she became forgetful and confused and it meant we couldn't leave her. I felt guilty if I went anywhere. It caused so much trouble within the family especially between my husband and me. When Mum became incontinent it was so hard. I had to wash her down, sometimes more than four times a day and sometimes she didn't recognise me and would be quite aggressive. I began to wish her dead. It was awful. I loved my mother so very much but I didn't recognise the person she was becoming.*

*Eventually we let her go into a care home where she died. Now I cannot forgive myself: I let my father down and I wanted my mother to die because I was selfish. It's all so destructive."*

It is not uncommon for the elderly parent to be the cause of many problems within the family and the death of a parent can leave many arguments and unresolved issues in its wake.

*"My sister hardly ever visited but since our mother died she seems to visit our parents' house a lot and is always talking about items of furniture that she'd like. I feel bitter about this because it was me who cared for mother for the last ten years. I made so many sacrifices, it's not fair."*

*"My brother is bullying me over the sale of our parents' home; he wants his share of the monies now. I feel like it's all too soon."*

*"My elder sister and I have argued since the day my father died; we even argued about the funeral arrangements."*

Most children have their parents with them throughout their childhood, teens and into adulthood and beyond, but the issues raised by the death of a parent will differ according to the age of the child. Of course, the impact can vary depending on how the parent died.

When a parent dies suddenly or unexpectedly there are many issues to be addressed, not least the circumstances of their death. Sudden death is usually as a result of illness, heart failure, accident, or, in rarer cases, suicide or murder.

A teenage boy suffered huge trauma when his mother died suddenly and unexpectedly from a brain haemorrhage. Not only was he shocked and traumatised by his mother's sudden death but he was overwhelmed with guilt and self-blame.

*"I feel really guilty. Mum said she had a headache that morning and asked me to bike to the shop to get painkillers. I refused and went out with friends to play football. When I got home Mum was in bed, really ill. I called a neighbour but by the time he arrived my Mum had died. It's my fault."*

He was initially unable to accept that his mother's death couldn't have been prevented, even if he had been to the shop and bought her the painkillers as she had asked. It is tempting to tell him that he isn't in any way to blame, to hush his words and to try to ease his grief and self-reproach. This, however, does not stop the lad from having such thoughts. Telling him not to feel guilty will not prevent or ease his private anguish. It was by allowing him space and time, and offering him a safe place to work through his private thoughts and grief, that eventually enabled him to move towards his acceptance of her death alongside the realisation that it was not caused by any of his actions nor was it preventable.

When a child is old enough to understand the circumstances of parental death there is often, in my experience, a reversal of roles. Children look to themselves for reasons, reproaching themselves for any 'bad' behaviour and they become caught in the 'should have', 'would have' or 'could have' trap; they feel guilty that they didn't save their parent, that they didn't or couldn't protect him or her. It is of the utmost importance that children are given the opportunity to talk honestly and frankly about their experience of the death of their parent. They need to be heard even when the thoughts and feelings are scary, uncomfortable to hear or see, or when there is temptation to fix or make the child feel better.

Children may also experience a sense of desertion and rejection. The parent didn't fight hard enough for life:

*"If he'd loved me, he wouldn't have left me."*

*"If she'd really cared about my sister and me, she'd have fought harder for life."*

*"Why didn't it happen to someone else's Mum?"*

*"What did I do wrong?"*

*"I feel really angry with my Dad because he seems to think that it's OK that he's going to die."*

A mother who was told she had terminal illness spent much time discussing her anticipated decline and death with her children. The children observing their mother's bravery felt that just as she and their father appeared to be managing and accepting so should they. The outward display of 'doing well', of accepting quietly all that was to come, enabled everyone, including the mother, to believe that it would be OK. Afterwards there were comments such as, "She did ever so well for the kids – so brave, so strong." Such statements placed the bereaved children under immediate pressure to play the 'being strong' game. They were expected to accept the death thing that was coming to take their mother forever, as if it was just another of life's mysteries, and to embrace it quietly for everyone's sake. But who is everyone?

Why, us, of course, those left behind, the observers, the helpers, friends, neighbours, acquaintances. It's so much easier for us to believe the children are 'doing well'. One of the children told me:

> *"I was so angry with myself, my Dad, the doctor, God, my Mum, her sister, everyone – even my best friend because I wanted it to be her Mum. I wanted to scream at my Mum to stop it – how could she leave me? My Dad said, 'Don't cry in front of Mum, it upsets her. We have to be strong.' I wanted to die with her. We were pretending it was OK. I cried every night, and every morning I thought, 'Will she die today?' Once I heard Dad and Mum crying together. I went into the room and they stopped and I felt excluded, so alone. We never talked about it. Mum tried to act like it was some place she was going, an adventure. I felt she left us long before she died. No-one knows how it is for me and they don't want to know."*

In this family the children were not allowed to the funeral. The husband/father was surrounded by supportive and well-meaning family and friends. The children were farmed out and told to be brave for their Dad and not to make a fuss. In the presence of others, the children, believing it to be a fitting tribute to how well their mother managed her illness and death, played the parts of 'doing ever so well' children, and so began their self-denial.

In my experience those who are terminally ill, whilst working through their own needs, anxieties and fears about their illness and approaching death, often feel they must make the acceptance of it and manageability easy for their families. They invest time in planning and putting affairs in order. In some cases, they grasp death by the throat by appearing in control until eventually overcome by it. Children can and do feel left out and disacknowledged. Their fear and loss are often left unaddressed. They are often denied the grieving with the dying parent for all that they will not share. Children's grief can feel too great, too big and overpowering. It says we have failed. Adults cannot fix everything. It steals away the security we wish our child to have, the belief in us that, as adults, we can protect, mend and take away the scary stuff of life.

It's distressing to observe the rawness of children's grief, and too often we fail them. We believe that by not involving them, by disacknowledging them, we make it easier for them to bear their grief. Children see and feel as we do and in so many ways they are more sensitive as they have not yet learnt to close down or cover up their feelings. The child has little life experience to draw upon and, in the very young, little understanding. By telling a young child that his or her parent has gone to be a bright star or to heaven to be with God also says it's better there; better than being here and better than being your parent. It is vitally important that children be told, regardless of the belief system, that there are no choices about death, that a mother or father would much prefer to stay with their children than to die, and that the child has not been rejected or deserted.

*"When my Dad was ill, my Mum and Dad talked
about it a lot. My Dad told me he loved me so
many times. He talked about his pain too and his
fear and sometimes we just cried together. I was 11
when he died and, although watching him so ill was
sad and distressing, I also knew he couldn't live on
and I knew how it really was. I felt part of it and
my Mum and I and my two brothers comforted each
other. It's two years now and we talk about Dad a
lot and all he went through. I know he couldn't live
on and that makes it easier in some ways to accept
his death."*

Clearly the family-sharing of the experience of this
teenager's father's death, though painful and traumatic,
also enabled acceptance. The honesty between the close
members of the family afforded them the opportunity
to communicate, to say things that perhaps might not
have been said and, importantly for the parent and
child, to share their grief together.

When a parent dies and the child or children are
young, there is a need for the remaining parent and or
close family members to keep open the channels of
communication, and availability of memorabilia. As
the child grows and develops understanding, he or she
can ask for and receive information about the deceased
parent. Time may seem far longer for the young. By
this I mean that the passage of one calendar year to a
child of eleven will present many changes, not only in
everyday or obvious expected ways, but in less notice-
able and more subtle ways as well. Children whose
parent dies when they are eleven will not only be
managing the obvious pain and grief that the death
has brought, but alongside it the massive changes to

themselves in growth, abilities and understanding. The way that a child of eleven is talked to, and the needs of a child of eleven, are very different from the needs and communication skills that are apparent in a child of thirteen.

As adults we do not change as quickly in these physical and mental ways. When we experience bereavement, we can be pretty sure how it will affect us, and that our memory of the person and of the death will remain constant. Children are often, and rightly, given information at the level that we perceive that they are capable of understanding. Children may be told about a parent's death and given what we believe they need at the time. However, in the succeeding months they continue to develop, and may need more information as their development proceeds.

Whilst working with bereaved teenagers, I became aware that many of them were experiencing a need to revisit and explore their parents' deaths as they grew older. Their needs and the comforts which they required at the time of the death were not the same as the needs as they grew older. As time passed they all seemed to say the same thing, "I knew my parent had died but I didn't realise then that it was forever."

A year to a child of eleven is an incredibly long time and over two or three years the changes that occur within the child are quite phenomenal. A girl whose mother died when she was eleven told me:

*"It's been three years since my Mum died and I try to remember her but it's really difficult. I live with my auntie. There are things I want to ask about Mum, but we don't talk about her often, and I don't feel I can ask much. When I try to remember her I*

*can't think of enough memories. I don't want my
auntie to be upset or to think she hasn't done a
good job looking after me. I think she thinks I'm
over it but I know I'll never get over it. In fact,
sometimes I feel worse than I did, and I can't
believe it's only three years since Mum died."*

Another teenager said:

*"It was five years ago, but I was just a little kid
then. I can't tell the family that I'm grieving what I
know I've lost now. They seem to be over it but I
feel like as I've got older I've woken up to it. My
Dad's death has affected everything. Sometimes I
feel so low just thinking about all the things I'm
missing with him and I struggle to get a picture of
him in my head or the sound of his voice. No-one
seems to realise how I feel. When Dad died I kind
of got through but as times passed and I've
changed, I've needed more. My Mum has started to
rebuild her life and I want her to be happy but I feel
like I need to talk more now. It's a very lonely place
to be."*

Clearly we need to be aware of the needs of children
who are bereaved and to realise that, for them, the
passage of time is not as much a healer as it might be
for the adult. The child's body growth, increasing
maturity and knowledge may bring further anguish.
My experience of bereaved children is that they are
largely disacknowledged. What we may feel is protection can be exclusive and isolating. Their grief may
need extensive space and time to revisit as changes
occur.

Change and lack of power after the death of a parent can also cause children to withdraw. They may feel that their feelings are selfish, or too demanding, but outwardly they may appear to be coping with their bereavement.

*"When my parents died in a car crash I was 13 years old. My elder sister and her partner and their children came to live at home and look after me. At first it was OK but then my sister's partner started to change things in the house, but no-one asked me. I felt like they had moved in on me. I was angry that they didn't seem aware of how I felt and guilty because everyone said they'd done a very unselfish thing coming to look after me, so I could stay in the house and at the same school and near my mates.*

*After a couple of months my sister started to get rid of things. She wanted to bring her own furniture in and this needed more space. They did let me keep one or two things that belonged to Mum and Dad but most of the stuff was taken away. It's three years since my parents died and I still feel out of place, lost. I sometimes feel like my life died when Mum and Dad died, like that's another life and now I am existing in one that doesn't fit. My sister gets really irritated with me and says I should be grateful, more appreciative. But I want to tell her that I feel like an intruder in my own home. It doesn't even look the same.*

*Soon I will leave school and get a job. I feel alone. No-one knows or understands that, when parents die, it changes everything forever and the ripples just go on. People think after three years I should be over it or at least feeling differently but I*

*still feel shocked; sometimes I think it can't be true.*
*Sometimes I sit very still in a room and try to hear*
*them: the familiar sound of Mum in the kitchen or*
*Dad watching TV. Then I get distressed because I*
*can't remember the sound of them. The other day I*
*realised that when Dad died I was only about 5 foot*
*tall, but now I'm 6 foot 2. If Dad were here I'd be*
*taller than him – that's hard to imagine."*

When a parent dies there are many, many changes in
store for the child. Some are obvious to all, but others
occur within the child's world and are not apparent to
the remaining parent or caregivers until the child speaks
about them. Some children do not speak at all, bearing
their grief alone. My observations of grieving children
are that they seem to be able to dip in and out of grief.
One moment they are immersed in its all-consuming
and painful reality, and in the next they are playing a
computer game or engrossed in a TV programme. This
swift mood change may to some observers seem fickle
or even perceived as lightweight grieving. But in my
experience this is simply how grief is. Individuals react
differently to their personal loss. That is acceptable and
needs acknowledgement. It's OK to do it your way.

Younger children are capable of decision making,
and they can benefit from being involved and given
choices where possible or practical. It is vital that in
the rush to give comfort and protection we do not
exclude emotions, or cause them to be stifled. We must
allow them space and time, so that they can begin to
adjust to a situation that has rocked their very core of
security. A sense of balance can be created by offering
them gentle acceptance of their individual experiences
and a willing, non-judgmental ear for as long as they

need it, alongside the security and continuum of life disciplines, required tasks, education and other boundaries.

The child's world is progressive, it changes daily. Experiences cause children to develop and grow. For some, traumatic experiences can cause stunting of growth. This is reversible as long as the child has the opportunity within a safe trusting relationship to explore and embrace all that the experience of grief brings to them. A child who has experienced the death of a parent needs ongoing opportunities to address what it means, and to reassess its impact on life as emotional needs change and grow alongside the changes in physical stature.

*"I've listed my losses since my Mum died. They are huge but they need to be because she was my Mum and that's how it is."*

My response to this is simply: "Yes, and for you that's exactly how it is."

# 3

# DEATH OF A SPOUSE OR PARTNER

The relationship between two people is unique, so the death of a person within that relationship, and the feelings experienced by the remaining partner, are as individual as the relationship itself. We all hide our true feelings beneath a shell, only showing people the parts of us that we wish them to see. It is only to our chosen partner that we reveal the real person beneath the façade. The whole truth about our relationship is known only to the two of us.

We assume that we know a great deal about the lives of family and friends, because we may have known them intimately for many years. Sometimes, however, we can find ourselves shocked by revelations about the private lives of people whom we thought we knew well.

Many bereaved partners have told me that they feel that assumptions have been made about their relationship by those on the periphery. Other people's perspective on their relationship can appear judgmental or devaluing. Our assumptions and interpretations may cause the remaining partner to feel unable to share grief and innermost feelings, and so become isolated. It may be difficult for the husband whose wife died of terminal illness to talk about his sense of relief, or for the surviving partner of a relatively new relationship to feel acknowledged as an important part of the deceased person's life.

In this chapter I hope to explore the diversity of grief for bereaved partners. When a partner dies, whether young or old, the hopes, dreams and plans for the couple's future are brought to an end. The death of the partner is the confirmation of mortality.

Death comes in many guises. Where it is sudden or unexpected, the bereaved partner may have to cope with many personal emotions, the grief of other family members and the sense that much has been left unsaid. It does not seem to matter how expected or planned a beloved partner's death is, the actuality can bring the sense that life is unfinished or passed too quickly. Men and women manage their grief in different ways and the differences in how they grieve are enormous.

There may also be secret areas in the life of the deceased which were not disclosed to partners or family members. Undisclosed financial affairs or debts may come to light, and, in some circumstances, unknown loved ones or other families, whose presence is only revealed after the death. Discovery of such hidden secrets can greatly add to the burden of grief of the surviving partner who may often feel unable to discuss them with anyone, but has to keep the knowledge locked inside, to be taken out and examined only when alone and vulnerable.

A man whose wife of fifteen years was diagnosed with terminal cancer told me that he felt he lost her the day her illness was confirmed.

*"I felt out of control – this sense of not being able to do anything to help her or change things, that we were both heading towards something so scary and there was nothing we could do. I felt angry, angry at her and at the doctors, angry that our lives were about to be messed up big time. I wanted to get away from it and, I feel ashamed to say it, I wanted her to die quickly. I didn't want her to go on dying slowly while I observed. I was scared of what lay ahead but not so much of after her death, strangely that didn't seem to come to mind much. I was scared of going through her illness with her. As time went by I felt excluded. She began this journey towards death and I was just there, not able to offer much at all. As more doctors and nurses became involved I felt useless. I talked to her about our lives, everyday stuff, but I couldn't join in her conversations about death. I felt angry that she seemed to accept it, although I knew there were no choices. As she grew more sickly she spent more time in hospital. There she befriended other people who seemed more able than I to communicate with her. I started to go out with the children alone. Our lives began to change. Before her illness I thought she would need me but there was nothing that I could do for her."*

The confirmation of his wife's illness brought with it a realisation that this wasn't something that could be resolved. He felt trapped by the illness and afraid of his own limitations. He was angry that life had suddenly changed, and the future that they planned was not going to happen. He was isolated by a sense of power-lessness and loss of control. He was ashamed of his vulnerability and fear of what was to come. His observations were that his wife had become part of a world from which he felt excluded, that medical professionals were now part of her life, and that the other patients were now her familiar and new social contacts. She had planned her funeral, talked about her hopes for the family after her death and appeared to be 'doing death well'. This led her husband to feel frustrated and more useless because he couldn't stop this death thing that had slipped unexpectedly through the back door whilst they were busy living. He couldn't protect her from it, bargain with it or change places with her. There were days when he wanted to leave and never come back, days when he wanted to shake her and make her fight it, and days when he wondered if today would be her last. The family were riding an emotional rollercoaster and no-one knew when or how it would stop.

*"As my wife grew more ill there was an air of impending death in the house, sometimes I felt I could smell it, touch it. Friends visited less frequently. I felt isolated and alone. Nurses were a welcome relief with their cups of tea and sensitivity but I couldn't tell them how I really felt. As my wife became more incapable I wished her dead. I looked at her once and thought, 'Who are you?' She didn't look like my wife any more. Letting her go to a hospital was not easy. I felt so guilty as they took her away. She had wanted to die at home but I couldn't go on with it any longer and, although I felt guilty, there were feelings of relief. It was coming to an end. For the next few days I sat with her. I felt guilty for not crying, for not desperately wanting her to keep going. I remember praying on every*

*breath that it would be her last.*

*After she had gone it seemed suddenly too soon. I begin to think all about how, for most of the time, I had distanced her and her death. I started to think about all I didn't do or hadn't said. I missed her. Sometimes I long for the closeness of her. I know it sounds bizarre but I have climbed into the wardrobe just to smell her clothes."*

The impact of discovering that your partner has a terminal illness is a shocking and often isolating experience. The need to understand and accept what is happening, alongside the fear and the knowledge of the changes to come, may be overwhelming. Often the focus is on the person who is terminally ill, and partners and other family members can feel alone and disregarded. The feelings that they are experiencing may be alien to them and emotions such as anger, resentment and self-pity may feel too awful to share.

Another husband talked about feelings of freedom after his wife's death, his contemplations about his attractiveness to other women, and a sense of excitement that he might meet someone else, swiftly followed by huge feelings of guilt because it felt like he was being unfaithful.

*"I think I got used to my wife not being here quite quickly and I feel guilty for that. I felt a sense of pleasure being able to do things and consider only myself. I missed her, of course, but I felt OK alone. In the beginning I tried to keep things the same (the garden, the household chores), but after a while I started to move things, change things and do things my own way. I enjoyed the changes.*

*I feel guilty about the garden mostly because my wife loved it so, and it was neat, but gardening was never my thing. I mean I only did it to please her. I sometimes wonder what the neighbours think."*

The change from 'we' to 'me' can be a very emotionally complicated process. Within relationships couples give up parts of themselves in order to gain togetherness. When a partner dies, there is conflict between the need to be the same, to continue without the partner and keep things going in the partner's absence, and with the need to find oneself. When death occurs in any circumstances it creates this permanent change within those it touches, characterized by the bereaved person's diversity of feelings – on the one hand feeling lost and needing continuity to keep the sense of security that existed because of the established relationship, but on the other hand the finding of new interests which are pertinent to you alone.

*"My husband bought this chair; he loved it and used to fall asleep in it every night in front of the telly. I never liked it, monstrous thing, it isn't even that comfy. I really want to get rid of it but I have this feeling that, if I do, I'm going against him. My daughter says, 'Oh Mum, you can't get rid of Dad's special chair.' "*

*"My wife said she wanted me to move on, maybe find someone else, not to be alone. It's like she's given permission but I still have these feelings of guilt. I was going to take off my wedding ring but it felt like I was leaving her and all that our marriage stood for behind."*

*"I always wanted to travel but my partner wouldn't;
now I can and I'm trying to get courage to go
alone."*

*"My husband and I had a rocky marriage. We
argued most days. I miss him so much. I wish we
hadn't spent so much time arguing, but I also feel
guilty because I feel better without those
arguments."*

The feeling of guilt is frequently experienced by those
who are bereaved, with many self-recriminations of
'should haves', 'would haves', 'could haves', 'wish I had
saids' and 'wish I hadn't saids'.

*"I was too busy that day. She said she didn't feel
well but I said, 'Oh get up and get about. You'll feel
better then.' I didn't kiss her goodbye. I didn't tell
her I loved her. I just stuck my head round the
bedroom door and said, 'You'll feel better if you get
up', then I said something like, 'See you later,' and
left. If I'd taken more care, if I'd waited with her, if
I'd been there, if, if, if. I ask her sometimes: 'Just
come back. It'll be different.' I know that sounds
stupid but sometimes I think it's all a cruel joke."*

This husband felt that by leaving his wife, by ignoring
her symptoms of illness, he was responsible for her
death. But even if he had stayed, his wife would not
have survived the sudden, massive heart attack that
killed her.

Bargaining with a deity or begging for the return of
the loved one is also common. The immediacy of being
alone, the lonely future stretching far, far ahead and the

cessation of all hopes, dreams or plans for the future are all that seem to be available to the bereaved partner at that time.

It is a common assumption to think that all deaths are mourned and a devastating blow to the surviving partner. One wife told me that, although she gave the impression of a grieving widow, she actually was glad her husband was gone from her life.

> *"My husband was a bully. For years he was aggressive and made our lives miserable. I often fantasized about life without him, thinking how much better it would be to be rid of him. I will cash the insurance policies, sell everything and do what I've always wanted: make a new life with my sister in Australia. I won't have to argue for a divorce any more."*

This woman experienced deep feelings of guilt because she was not as devastated by the loss of her husband as other people assumed she was. We spent a lot of time working through her turbulent relationship with her husband, and her frustration and anger with herself for not dealing with it while he was alive.

Another common assumption made by 'outside' people is that elderly people who have been married for many years accept the death of a partner as a natural occurrence. Therefore the bereaved partner is not the recipient of as much consideration and understanding as a younger widow/er. People justify these assumptions using such phrases as, "Oh well, he/she was 70/80/90. He/she had a good innings."

A woman of 80, whose husband died unexpectedly whilst asleep, told me:

*"We were together forever. I can't quite believe it was 63 years, it has flitted by all too soon. I can't imagine going on without him. No amount of time would have been long enough for us. I wasn't ready for it yet and I want to slap those who keep saying he had a good innings."*

Society treats the young widow very differently from the older widow, but who is more deserving of our compassion? The young widow gains sympathy for her perceived loss and for the years she did not have with her husband. The older widow is the recipient of such comments as, "Well, you had a long time together", but which of them is going to find grieving easier, or death more acceptable? The older widow has a confirmation of the finality of life and her sense of isolation and loneliness can seem unbearable. Her family's lack of regard and understanding causes her greater distress and depression, all largely unacknowledged, because after all "they had had a good innings"!

Who is the judge of how long is a 'good innings'? Does age alter the depths of emotion and feelings? Do we become less sensitive to loss when those we love and are long-standing parts of our lives take their leave and depart? Does age bring quiet acceptance of our own mortality? If we were married for a hundred years would that make letting go easier?

There may be the nagging suspicion that perhaps the aged do not march joyfully on leaving those they love behind, and that those they love do not willingly accept their passing. Perhaps it is this which keeps us uttering such banal statements as, "He had a good innings" or "Life was very difficult for her after the last stroke." All too often assumptions are made and the true feelings of those grieving the loss of their cherished partner are neither heard nor acknowledged.

A loving partnership can also involve those who were not married but committed within a relationship. Following the death of one partner, the surviving partner can often find his or her position disregarded. In law, perhaps, the blood family of the deceased person may take precedence as 'next of kin', but both emotionally and morally a partner needs to have the relationship with the deceased person acknowledged and considered. A young fiancé of a woman killed in an accident told me:

> *"I had no say at all about anything. I wanted to arrange the funeral and I wanted her buried nearby but her family made those decisions. I feel angry that they said, 'You're young; you'll meet someone else. Thank goodness you weren't married or there weren't any children.'"*

Words of comfort and hope for the future, offered by people who mean to be kind, can unintentionally trivialise the depth of commitment between the partners. They may try to be positive and show the bereaved person that there is a future, laying it out with enthusiasm and optimism, but who are they trying to reassure? Themselves, maybe? The focus for the grieving partner in this relationship was the loss of his beloved fiancée. He still needed to acknowledge his loss of being part of a couple, and the loss of their future together.

Well-meaning people, trying to comfort a bereaved person, sometimes say, "Well, at least you don't have children." They don't realise that this lack of a tangible proof, that once there was enough love between them to have a child together, is yet another twist of the knife in the raw wound of grief. It can be thought that a future life may be less complicated because the couple didn't have a family. The assumption often is that youth gives the bereaved time to heal and it may be easier to make a future for someone who carries no outward baggage from the past. This may be true, but in the immediacy of grief, the thought of any future, let alone with a new partner, is unthinkable.

*"When my partner died I felt as though everything went with him, I know this might sound strange, but I'm also grieving the children we often talked about having. We used to talk about the future and having a family, we even gave the children, we hoped one day to have, names. I feel they have died too. I can't tell anyone this. They'd think I was crazy."*

Partners of the deceased often struggle to gain recognition of their place within the life of their loved one. The devaluation of the relationship can cause added anguish and create a greater need for acceptance. Sometimes there is no recognition or acceptance of the partnership from the relations of the deceased.

*"We were together for just over a year. We'd just moved in together. I feel as though I'm not important. My girlfriend's family said they are coming to collect her things, I feel powerless."*

A married man who had been having an affair with another woman told me:

*"I feel like this is my punishment. I have been denied everything."*

He was faced with grieving alone, unable to share his loss with anyone. He clearly felt that his deceit was punished by the death of the woman he loved and exclusion from the closed circle of shared grief.

Secrets may be revealed about a person after death. Letters, diaries and even texts can offer revelations of thoughts and feelings, both past and present, that can be either comforting or the cause of added distress to the bereaved partner and their family.

*"After her death I started to go through old photos and keepsakes. I knew she kept a diary but I wasn't expecting it to be so intimate or so revealing. Initially I found comfort in her words but there were also graphic accounts of arguments, her thoughts about me, and her anger and, in some passages, her hatred and plans to leave me. These were very distressing. I feel angry with her for dying and for not being here to talk this through – I'm just left to deal with it."*

It is very important not only to face the impact of any negative discoveries, but also to accept them. It is also necessary to maintain balance, and for the bereaved partner to realise that some of the writings in the diaries were loving and comforting for him, whilst others caused him distress. The reality was that this was the truth about this relationship as the deceased saw it. As human beings we often focus on the negative aspects of a situation and decry the positive aspects as those having less importance.

Those who are emotionally devastated cannot find the capacity to rationalise alone, often erring on the side of self-recrimination. It is very beneficial to encourage exploration of the whole relationship, trying to accept both the imperfections and the glorious moments, in order to create a balance of perspectives.

## Sex and New Relationships

There are many instances where the newly bereaved have disclosed that they felt the need for sexual satisfaction within a very short time of the death of a partner, and felt guilty for having thoughts at such a time.

> *"I feel so ashamed that after my wife's funeral I relieved myself by masturbating. I went to bed and just had this need for comfort. I haven't masturbated for ages, but it felt overpowering, afterwards I felt guilty. I seem to need this like a comforter."*

> *"I don't understand why I have this need. Sometimes when I think about my wife I feel guilty and if I think about other things – fantasise – I feel guilty too."*

These feelings and actions are not unusual or disturbing as the craving for comfort is, I believe, the driving force behind the sexual need. Young children often rock or caress their genitals when they are distressed, which seems to provide fulfilment of their need for comfort. These feelings can resurface when we feel threatened, stressed or traumatised and all of these emotions are very strong during the period of grieving, and self-gratification can be comforting. Sometimes people disclose that they have sought comfort from another person and feel deep regret or confusion about their need and actions. Attachments can be formed to those involved, for instance with nurses who may have been closely involved with the dying person and are perceived having a sympathetic and caring nature. A nurse may become the confidante of the very private and personal thoughts of the surviving partner and, consequently, may become a focus of his attention.

The bereaved are vulnerable and often emotionally insecure. Their need for contact with others can be misinterpreted and lead to complicated situations beyond their capacity to manage.

*"I nursed my husband at home until he died. His brother and I had never been close and I certainly never thought of him in any way other than as my brother-in law. In my husband's last days I found his brother so supportive. After his death I longed to be held and I don't quite know how or why but I ended up with my brother-in law. He stayed over with me and I just so needed the affection.*

*Now I feel guilty, I don't know how to live with myself. I just feel like I've sullied my husband's memory."*

*"I was so lonely. My neighbour, a single mum, had been amazing while my wife was in hospital. She's a really lovely person. I did find her attractive – who wouldn't? When my wife was ill she sat with me till the early hours, just keeping me company, and I knew I was getting attached to her. I even fantasised about asking her out. Anyway we have slept together just once and straight away afterwards I*

*regretted it. I feel like I've been unfaithful, but I
needed someone so much. Now I can't bear to see
her. It's all too unmanageable."*

When we are in crisis and vulnerable to our emotions,
we may be unable to think as clearly as we usually do.
We may make decisions that we regret. The period
following the death of a beloved partner is a time of
immense emotional turmoil. These are not 'normal'
times and our needs and desires can be in a confusing
jumble. Those who are the focus of attention of a
bereaved partner need to be aware of this. Whatever
needs the bereaved may have at this stage, concern and
regard for his or her vulnerability still need to be the
main motivating factor whilst in his or her company.
Jumping into an intimate encounter or relationship with
a bereaved person in the early days after such a loss can
be the cause of greater devastation, added complications, and anguish, not only for those immediately
involved but also for the extended family.

Family and friends may sit in judgment on the
remaining partner. There can be complete confusion
about how things ought to be. Often friends and family
try to jolly the bereaved out of grief, invitations here
and there and introductions to new friends. However,
the bereaved who takes a new partner may be judged
and talked about as though he/she is doing this too
soon, but what, and in whose opinion, is 'too soon'?

The Victorians had a set period for mourning to show
'proper respect' to the dead. The length of mourning
depended on your relationship to the deceased. The
different periods of mourning dictated by society were
expected to reflect your natural period of grief. Widows
were expected to wear full mourning for two years.

Everyone else presumably suffered less – for children mourning parents or vice versa the period of time was one year, for grandparents and siblings six months, for aunts and uncles two months, for great uncles and aunts six weeks, for first cousins four weeks.

These days there is no set length or correct pattern to a period of mourning. Yes, you do need time, space and support, followed by a gentle introduction back to a different and perhaps intimidating life which, for you, has changed from the familiar ways of the past. If this future does include a new partner, then, as long as this happens in your time and when you are ready, welcome the opportunity.

**Supporting a Bereaved Partner**
If you take the decision to support a bereaved partner, then you first need to ask yourself why you are seeking to support this person. Be aware of your own personal needs and be guarded about your motives. Bereaved people need to work through their feelings before they are capable of thinking about another relationship. So, even where you feel physically attracted to them, try to use your capacity to manage your feelings. Allow time for them to complete their pathway through the grieving process. If you hope a relationship will eventually develop, it will benefit from time, space and a more emotionally solid foundation.

*"I met my new partner almost a year after my wife's death. I feel very anxious about any sexual relationship. I enjoy cuddling her but I just feel it's wrong to take it further. I don't think I am capable of sexual intimacy with anyone else yet. I do fancy her but I just feel like I'm being*

*unfaithful. Also, I know it sounds silly but I keep thinking of my wife watching me and I don't want to hurt her. I sometimes get aroused but can't bring myself to orgasm either; it just feels wrong."*

Just as increased sex drive is not unusual after bereavement, the anxiety and stress which are usual at this time can cause a lack of sex drive, or impotency. Feelings of guilt and unfaithfulness, and thoughts about the deceased partner and feeling that he/she may be watching are also usual, often unspoken for fear of ridicule. Communicating these thoughts and feelings to a trusted friend or counsellor can help tremendously with the manageability of grief, and self-permission to live alongside loss.

### Single Parenting Children

*"I am trying so hard to keep things together; I try not to get upset in front of the children. At first I just kept busy but now I'm finding it hard to get motivated. Sometimes I feel angry with her for leaving us, for leaving me with the kids. I can't do it all alone. Then I get angry with myself."*

*"I feel so totally alone. I cry at night when my kids are in bed. I can't let them see me cry, I think they'd be scared if they knew how I feel. I'm worried too about money and how we're going to manage. I sometimes wish I could just walk away. It's so hard, much harder than I ever thought it would be without him. I don't want people to know I'm not doing as well as they think."*

Becoming a single parent through bereavement is incredibly hard, physically, mentally and emotionally. Many newly bereaved partners tell me they feel exhausted, that they hide their emotions fearing to let their children see their devastation. They are anxious about coping, doing things the right way and appearing to be managing. The stifling of feelings and the constant anxiety drains their energy and adds to their sense of isolation. Sometimes the remaining parents feel they have to keep things to a certain standard, fulfil the role of the deceased parent and go beyond the needs of their bereaved child in order to compensate. They fear communicating their own grief because often they fear letting go, losing control of themselves and not being able to recover. The pressure to see their children through grief is their main priority. Sometimes overprotection of children, and the belief that the children should not see the bereaved parent's distress, can be the cause of breakdown of real communication within the family.

Children can be more aware than we realise, and they too can hide their feelings in order to protect the remaining parent. This quickly becomes a vicious circle: the children trying to protect their parent, the parent trying to protect the children and thus no-one speaks.

*"My Dad seems to be OK. He doesn't talk much about Mum. He sometimes cries but never in front of us. My aunties say we must all be strong. I never talk much about Mum because it just upsets everyone but I would like it if Dad and I could talk about her, even if we are sad."*

By allowing children to see our pain and our grief we reassure them that they too can express their feelings.

They do not have to protect us from their scary grief. By observing that sadness in others is acceptable, they too can share their own feelings. It is important for families to communicate and for the deceased parent to be talked about and mourned. We cannot protect those we love from death, or from feeling its impact, but by communication we can help them to manage and accept their loss.

## Making Changes

We are often not aware of small, subtle everyday changes until suddenly they have happened, and we realise that something is no longer as it was before. Making changes can feel very uncomfortable. Some changes may be inevitable, necessary for the everyday management/functioning of the family. Other changes may be made by choice and these often cause mixed feelings. On one hand, there may be pleasure in change and, on the other, guilt, because those changes take a little more of the loved one away.

*"After my husband's death I decided we ought to move nearer to my parents. We had only moved to this area because of his work. I longed to be near my Mum and Dad; I needed their support with my baby.*

*I wish I hadn't rushed it now. I feel alien in my new house and I miss familiar things. It feels like my whole world has changed."*

*"I decided to redecorate our room. I don't know why but I just wanted to pack up my wife's things and change everything. I feel lost now, like I've pushed her out completely and I miss the sense of her in our room."*

Sometimes, well-meaning family or friends may insti-
gate change, believing that it can help the bereaved
partner. The choice, the decision to change, needs to be
thought through carefully and nothing done in haste. It
is vitally important that the remaining partner and
children are consulted about any change and that they
are comfortable with it.

> *"In spite of the attempts of family and friends, and
> their kind offers to sort through my wife's clothing,
> I am not ready to do it. I want to keep her things
> where they are; our children like to see her things
> around. We talk about her, we miss her, we know
> that she was here with us. I know a time will come
> when we are ready, but why don't others allow us to
> just be as we are?"*

Why do we try to encourage the bereaved to pack up
their loved one's possessions? Why do we believe they'll
feel better for it? Is it our own awkwardness about the
belongings of the dead that causes us to rush to offer to
pack them for others? The physical evidence of his or
her existence – the coat or shoe that will never be worn
again, the bag or briefcase that will no longer be carried
– all remind us that their owner is no longer here.

It does perhaps reinforce the fact that we are only a
friend or family member. We can only observe the grief
of the family. We cannot make it better or make the
grief go away. So, we encourage the packing up, the
moving on. We discourage the lingering. We bring out
the 'doing well blanket'. Oh good, they've changed the
house, gone on holiday, bought a new car – they seem to
be getting over it, they appear to be 'doing well'and that
is comfortable. We can accept that. We have helped

them achieve **our** goal – getting on with their life.

But, of course, the truth is that we cannot run from the pain of bereavement. Holidays, cars, decorating and change do not make it easier or go away. It is only time (measured in seconds, minutes, hours, days, weeks, months and years), coupled with the opportunity to communicate and feel heard, that will eventually help the bereaved work their way through the turmoil of grief towards the relative calm of acceptance.

# 4

# WHEN A CHILD DIES

**Death before Birth**
The confirmation of pregnancy can be the most fulfilling and exciting moment of a woman's life. The feelings of anticipation and expectation generated at this time are unlike any she has experienced previously.

Some pregnancies are not so welcome and, for some, the news may be devastating. They may decide to terminate the pregnancy, either for reasons of a personal nature or on medical advice. Some women experience a sense of relief following their termination, but for others it may be an emotionally painful experience. Whatever the decision or circumstances, all women need the opportunity to acknowledge their feelings and address any issues raised by the decision.

When a woman is glad to be pregnant, and happy with her condition, she begins to plan for her child and for the bright and exciting future ahead for her and her family. The baby growing inside her may already be given a personality. More of the expectant mother's attention will be paid to other people's children, as, in her own mind, she relishes her impending motherhood.

Some expectant mothers feel an almost instantaneous connection with their growing child, and women who miscarried as early as 10 or 12 weeks have told me that they already knew in their minds what sex their baby was, and how he or she would look. Miscarrying a baby is a traumatic experience, both emotionally and physically. Many women often feel further distress by hearing their baby referred to as a 'foetus', a 'cluster or bunch of cells', a 'miscarriage' or a 'missed abortion'. The medical professionals' usage of correct but insensitive language can make the grieving mother feel disregarded. Alongside her need to acknowledge the little life that was developing inside her, she may be experiencing feelings of failure, guilt, self-blame and redress.

*"When I started bleeding, I went to bed, I tried tilting my body so that my lower half was higher, I thought that might hold him in. I couldn't stop it. I just bled and I felt so alone. I sat on the loo just crying. It seemed too awful that my baby was disappearing down the toilet. The doctor said he'd admit me for a scrape. That word felt so brutal. No-one talked about my baby like he was a baby, but to me he was very real. I used to look at books with photographs of developing babies and think, 'Ah this week his little hands are growing.' I don't think anyone knew what to say; someone said, 'It's probably for the best,'. . . I felt alone. I kept thinking, 'Why me? What had I done wrong?', then I thought it was because I'd had a drink at my friend's wedding. It was only one drink but I wish I'd been more careful. I called my baby Steven. I can't just forget him. Giving him a name makes it*

*easier somehow. Although everyone else thinks he
was just a blob, I regarded him, loved him, wanted
him and I won't forget him."*

The misuse of language can cause added pain and
distress to the bereaved parents and, in particular, the
mother. Words of support offered by well-meaning
friends and family, such as "You'll have another
baby", or "It's nature's way", may make the mother
feel that her loss is not being recognised as a bereavement. Her grief often remains unexplored and in
isolation. The hormone levels in her body are still
telling her that she is pregnant. Her body's return to a
pre-pregnancy state can take some time and cause side
effects.

*"I was thrilled when I was pregnant . . . it was my
first time and I felt so special. I was so shocked
when the doctor said he couldn't see a heartbeat on
the scan and in one moment my world was
devastated. I wanted to get home and be with my
partner but the doctor admitted me for a D & C
(Dilation and Curettage). I had never had one of
those before. He said I'd had a missed abortion . . .
I didn't understand his language really. I was
admitted to hospital and in the next bed to me was
a woman who was pregnant with twins and on the
other side was a young girl who had had a
termination. I was in the middle. I was alone and I
had to wait until morning for them to take me to
theatre. I felt like everything was out of control and
I had no choice. I didn't ask too many questions
because I thought they'd think I was a nuisance.
Strangely I didn't feel any different . . . I still felt*

*pregnant. I wondered if they'd made a mistake. I
was shaking and sobbing as I went down to theatre
and I felt totally patronised by the nurses who
referred to me as a big, brave girl. Afterwards a
doctor said my baby had died at least two weeks
before and that this happens sometimes . . . I should
go home and in a while try again.*

*What about my baby . . . where was it? I felt
pretty helpless and as if asking anything was
inappropriate. It was important though for me to
know about my baby. I couldn't see it but I wanted
to know where they had disposed of it. I was
haunted by these thoughts of it being kept in a jar
somewhere. I felt very low. I couldn't talk to anyone
about it and as days went by I began to feel as
though I was engulfed by black. I lost interest in
everything and I couldn't cry. I felt numb. A vicar
came to see me and I told him I wanted to know
about my baby. I was 14 weeks gestation when it
died. The hospital told him that they put the
remains of my baby in the sluice. I was very
distressed but then the vicar said the sluice would
eventually go to the sea and in that I found a little
hope. I was depressed for almost a year and life lost
its joy for me. I will never forget how I felt. I have
two children aged 15 and 13 now, but I feel I really
had three and still think of that baby and the life it
never had."*

Many thoughts and feelings are so often left unspoken.
The lack of acknowledgement and of importance may
lie beneath the surface causing resentment and stress
within the relationship. Whilst acknowledging that both
partners are affected by the death of their unborn child,

the feelings of the woman are governed by the hormones released in her body during pregnancy. She suffers the ongoing symptoms that can affect her in ways that her partner may not be able to understand or relate to. A woman may yearn to be pregnant again almost immediately, and experience a sense of frustration if told by doctors to wait a while, or if her partner seems hesitant.

> *"After we lost the baby my partner was really supportive for the first few weeks, but after that I could tell he was getting fed up with me talking about it. I was still feeling so empty, so sad, and so very cheated. He said he felt sad – sorry that we weren't going to have the baby after all but that we would have a baby one day. I really wanted to talk about this baby, the one I was expecting. I know people say that they aren't babies at 14 weeks, but I felt like mine was. I was sure it was a boy and I used to look at pictures in magazines and try to imagine what he'd look like. I felt I'd lost my child and no-one really wanted to know. In the end I just kept my feelings in. It took ages for me to fall pregnant again, and I have a daughter now aged three, but I want my unborn child to be acknowledged too."*

For some couples the desire for a child can become the focus of their life. This often brings added stresses and pressures to the relationship, and in particular to the sexual aspect of the relationship. Anxieties about conception can create impotence or cause once enjoyable and relaxed lovemaking to feel contrived, planned and clinical.

*"We used to have such a fantastic sex life . . . it was spontaneous and exciting. Since losing our baby we have been trying for another and 'doing it' at certain times – I've been taking my temperature and keeping a chart so we know when I'm ovulating. My partner often finds arousal difficult. I have felt like we are not as close . . . I didn't expect this to happen and now he says he thinks we should stop thinking about another baby for a while . . . I can't. It's causing lots of arguments. No-one seems to understand."*

The loss of a baby in the early weeks can cause an expectant mother to blame herself or experience a sense of failure. It is important to explore these feelings and to acknowledge the experience and its impact on the mother, the relationship and the ripple effect on all areas of life.

*"I had just attended my first ante-natal class . . . I was 14 weeks and my friend was also pregnant. We had planned to do so much together and life seemed complete. When I lost the baby, she was upset and afraid for herself. I felt angry that she was concerned about herself, her pregnancy. It seemed so unfair that this happened to me. She stopped coming round – she told my husband that she found it hard, that she felt guilty for still being pregnant. I was glad that she stopped calling. I didn't want to hear about her or see her getting bigger. It was like part of my life was taken away . . . my plans. Also I noticed other pregnant mums and thought, 'Why couldn't it have been you?' I felt guilty about that and angry too."*

This might be a mother's first experience of loss, and the extent and depth to which she is impacted will depend, not only on the level of support and understanding she receives, but on past experiences. Her recovery may be helped or hindered by the care she receives at this crucial time. Bereavement can often cause other fears to rise to the surface and may be a trigger for the release of past emotional turmoil.

I receive many letters from women expressing their innermost thoughts and feelings; women whose babies have not survived into life, and who are holding their feelings of loss within themselves. They write of their grief at the lack of society's acknowledgement of their child's existence and death. They bewail the lack of understanding of friends, family, neighbours and work colleagues during the struggle to come to terms with their loss. They portray their overwhelming feelings of emptiness, arising from some of them feeling that a part of them has died with their child. All deaths, both before and after birth, need acknowledgement and acceptance, for only then can those who are bereaved feel they have permission to mourn.

*"I started to get this really bad pain in my stomach. I phoned the doctor. He said that it sounded like food poisoning and if I wasn't better in 24 hours to call him again. Within a few hours I knew I was having contractions – I was seven months pregnant. I phoned my husband, but by the time he got home they had stopped. I went to my doctor; he couldn't find a heartbeat and admitted me to hospital. My baby had died but I had to deliver it.*

*I was so shocked and I couldn't believe that my baby had died. I thought they had made a mistake.*

*I was hoping that once labour started they'd tell me
it was OK. I had lots of pain relief and the staff at
the hospital were very kind. After just a few hours
my baby son slipped silently into the world. He
looked perfect. I didn't want them to take him to
perform an autopsy but they said they would need
to establish why he died. I was horrified that my
baby, with his perfect little body, was going to
endure yet more. I was so alone, so useless and
cheated. The hospital took photos of him for me
and I named him but they didn't offer anything
else."*

In many hospitals there seems to be the assumption that
the reason why a patient doesn't ask a question is
because she doesn't want to know the answer. My
experience is that often the patient does want to know,
but perhaps does not know how to ask for information.
Patients are frightened that these capable and efficient
people who are caring for them may think that they are
a nuisance, that they are morbid or strange, and that
they may not like them if they make a fuss.

All people are individuals with their own ways of
feeling and behaving. Yet we expect them all to conform
to acceptable and emotionally strait-jacketed behaviour
at a time of enormous mental and physical turmoil and
distress. Perhaps it is because we are afraid that, if we
experience the real and raw emotion of another person's
distress, we will be unable to control or contain our
feelings which will then escalate and magnify beyond
our control.

Some hospitals are only too aware of the depth of
grief and distress experienced by bereaved 'death before
birth' parents and are willing to spend time with them.

They try to answer their questions honestly without recourse to jargon, and consider their requests sympathetically. Unfortunately, though, there are other hospitals which, perhaps because they suffer staff and money shortages, have neither the time or facilities to provide this comfort. The bereaved 'death before birth' parents leave the hospital, taking a huge number of unanswered questions and confused thoughts home with them.

## Birth and Death
In some circumstances a woman who has had a healthy pregnancy may tragically lose her child during labour, or due to complications in vitro (inside the womb) her child dies just prior to or during labour.

For these mothers the complications and trauma of giving birth and watching their baby die are so very distressing and many tell me that they felt alone, misunderstood and unsupported. The mother is often returned to the maternity ward where she may then endure the added distress of hearing other mothers give birth, and the cries of their healthy and living babies.

Most hospitals now recognise and accept that the bereaved parents may wish to be with their stillborn baby and for them to have time alone in this way is extremely important. Many hospitals encourage mothers to hold their deceased baby, take photos, handprints or footprints and allow the parents private time with their child. It is not unusual for mothers to want to dress their baby, cuddle it and love it. The tangible evidence of photographs, handprints or footprints gives the parents, in the months and years ahead, confirmation of their child's existence and that their experience was real.

*"Everything was fine with the pregnancy. I had been
so well and felt really good, unlike my first
pregnancy where I felt ill most of the time. When I
think back I did feel uncomfortable about going
over my date. I was a little anxious but my GP said
it was fine and I did feel good. Things just went so
very wrong. I still don't know exactly what
happened. It seems the cord was around my baby's
neck and she died before they could deliver her.
Afterwards I held her, so tiny and perfect. I dressed
her and wrapped her in the little pink outfit and
blanket that I had hoped to take her home in. I felt
very calm at the time; I remember thinking it was a
dream. I tucked her under my arm and slept. When
I woke up I thought, 'I've had my baby', and I felt
excited. Then I started to realise that she had died
and there she was alongside me: blue and cold.*

*The worst part was leaving her there in the
hospital. I put her tiny body into her crib and said
goodbye but I just couldn't bear to leave her.
Looking at her lying there I tried to take in every
detail. I thought I have to make this last me a
lifetime. I told her I was so sorry and I loved her.
Finally a nurse and my husband took my arms and
turned me away. I could barely walk. The pain with
each step that I felt as I left her alone there in the
hospital was agonizing; my heart really felt as
though it were breaking."*

Leaving hospital can bring forth a mixture of complicated feelings. The expectant parents had entered the
building with the expectation of new and family life.
The building may now feel like a place of limbo and
disconnection where the reality of all that has

happened has still to be accepted.

It can feel safe within the hospital. The reality of going home without the baby can be overwhelming. Leaving hospital empty-armed and childless is the first, full impact of reality. Some parents have told me that they would have liked to have taken their baby home with them.

> *"I wanted to bring her home, to keep her at home*
> *until the funeral. I just wanted her to feel wanted,*
> *not discarded 'Baby Jones'. I wanted my little girl*
> *to have known that she had a home, a crib, a room,*
> *a family. It felt bizarre to think this. I didn't*
> *mention it, not even to my husband. A long while*
> *after, he said he thought about that too, but we both*
> *didn't share our thoughts because we felt that they*
> *would be considered morbid, that the hospital would*
> *refuse us the right, or that they might think we were*
> *crazy."*

Many bereaved parents have told me of their feelings of not having any rights, of their baby becoming in some way the property of the hospital or funeral director, of being unable to ask for more time with their child and of wanting to do as they wish with their baby including taking it home.

There must come a time when we, as a community of considerate and caring people, start to help our fellow human beings to work through the acceptance of the death of their loved one and their tragedy in their own way, without inflicting on them our assumptions or judgments. In some hospitals, counselling/support services are available and it is beneficial for the bereaved parents to have an opportunity to talk through their feelings, both before and after leaving hospital. Where this service is not available, supportive and listening family and friends can be of huge assistance.

It is very important to recognise that the couple whose child has died have experienced circumstances which are beyond their control and where they had no choices whatsoever. They must be encouraged to make choices, and to feel that some areas of their life are still within their control, even in these early grief-stricken days where the energy to make choices and decisions may be limited.

There may also be issues surrounding mother and child care during the final stages of gestation and in labour, e.g. on-going investigations and legal procedures and evidence may need to be sought by solicitors and other professionals. This coupled with the trauma, the tragic death, stresses and anxieties can affect the relationship between the couple. Feelings of resentment, failure, guilt, anger and depression are all usual, but communication between the couple can become fraught. There are many aspects that may change the relationship, not least the loss of the way things were, and the lack of hope for the future, coupled with the loss of self.

*"I go over and over it. I comb through every detail. I lie in bed every night thinking it through. Sometimes I try to focus on one of the doctors or a nurse. I wonder, 'Did they cause it to happen?' I think about my wife and sometimes I blame her for not being more able; if she had worked harder at the delivery . . . I hate myself for blaming anyone but there has to be an answer – doesn't there?"*

*"I feel a failure. I let my baby down. I should have told them to perform a caesarean. I should have known. I should have protected my baby. I hate the nurses – when I think it through I keep hearing this one nurse talking about a night out and I feel angry that she was not as involved with me."*

*"I want to hate the midwife who made a mistake in my delivery but I can't. Right now I feel so sad it's like my heart beats pain and is heavy."*

The couple may at first be comforting to each other, both feeling isolated and lost within their nightmare but as time passes their individual feelings of loss rise to the surface.

*"I feel cheated. At first I felt grief for our baby, now I feel grief for me. I don't feel the same any more about anything and my world feels uncertain. I feel lost."*

*"I couldn't talk to her, tell her what I really felt; it was too devastating, too punishing. I hated her, but I felt such sadness for her too, all at the same time. It was totally inexplicable to feel such deep feelings of hate and resentment for the woman I loved and felt so devastated for. I also felt I'd let her down, failed to protect her. In my hating feelings, I wanted to leave her, to run away from it all. All I had planned and worked for was stolen. I often looked at her and thought she had changed. I couldn't understand the diversity of my feelings. I felt like I didn't want her near me. Not only had she changed emotionally but physically she put on a lot of*

*weight and she wasn't bothered, it seemed, about how she looked. I felt less of a man. I felt people thought I was a failure. I thought they were secretly blaming me. She was a living reminder of what we'd been through. At the same time I felt totally sad for her, protective of her vulnerability and, though unable to show it, a deep sense of love and guilt too for all she'd been through.*

*Our relationship was changed forever. We had been so very excited about the baby, so happy, in love, a future that seemed great. Now we were both devastated, lost and unable to communicate. I was so angry at everything but unable to put it anywhere."*

*"At first we were close. There was a time, for a while, of huge understanding. I felt cared for; he was so attentive and comforting.*

*But then it started to change, I felt it was my fault. I also felt angry with him for not doing more at the birth but I knew in reality there was nothing. I felt empty, loveless, like when our baby died, part of me died too. He didn't want to talk about it. I used to go and sit by the crib and gaze for hours trying to remember every detail of our baby. My hospital bag was still unpacked. I just couldn't put things away. He used to get irritated with me. I felt like everything died with our baby – even us. There seemed to be no hope."*

The death of the baby had changed everything for this couple. Initially they were able to comfort each other, and the support and understanding of those involved enabled them to grieve openly. It was acceptable for them to be shocked, tearful and at a loss, but as time progressed the divisions in their once easy relationship became more apparent as the reality of their baby's death affected every part of their life.

Family and friends of the couple can help by making themselves available and simply listening to them talk. Professional grief counselling, either individually or as a couple, would be of huge benefit. Everything has changed. It is important that this is acknowledged so that the relationship can move forward.

The death of a child is so life changing, and the pressures felt by the child's parents are so enormous, that many couples cannot see the way forward together. A separation following bereavement is not uncommon. The bereaved couple, who may be experiencing an overwhelming sense of failure as parents, now have to cope with appearing as a failure as a couple as well. They may try and protect family and friends from the truth and become burdened with the added stresses of putting on an appearance of managing their circumstances and emotions. Their feelings are very real, but their difficulty is in accepting the lack of control or choice in the recent turmoil of their life.

Even couples who are able to talk openly to each other about their emotions, and manage to retain their relationship, need acknowledgement of their trauma and its ongoing ripple effect. They need to forge, on the foundations of this communication, a stronger and closer bond.

Experiences change us and alter our perceptions. The death of someone we loved makes us question all that we trust and hold dear. Plans are changed as future hopes come crashing down around our ears. Death is common to each and every one of us, but each experience is unique and creates change within us.

**Funerals**

Where the parents hold religious convictions, church leaders will generally visit the parents if requested and, in most cases, a blessing can be given to the baby. The bereaved parents then have the difficult task of arranging the funeral and also the dilemma of whom to invite. It can feel uncomfortable for those invited to such a funeral, especially where other couples are expectant or have infants or small children. This can sometimes create a breakdown in relationships with friends.

It is important that the bereaved parents do things the way they wish. The most helpful family member or friend will be the one who asks, "What do you want to do and how can I help you to do it?"

If the couple wish to bring their baby home, the funeral director will advise them about keeping their baby until the funeral. Keeping the baby at home can be extremely beneficial as it provides the parents with private opportunity to be with their child. It takes away the feeling that the child belongs to the hospital or that they might be being observed or judged. It permits other members of the family to share time with the baby and an opportunity, depending on their age and understanding, to grasp what has happened.

Preparing the baby and experiencing feelings of wanting to make him or her comfortable or cosy are usual. Special outfits can be chosen and it can be a comfort to the mother to care for her child in this way. Photographs might be taken and letters written and placed in the baby's casket. Parting with the baby should not be a rushed event and parents should be encouraged and allowed as much private time as they feel they want. No amount of time is ever enough, but they will be aware of eventually having to say goodbye to their child.

The parents may find comfort in the funeral service and the presence of family and friends, but in the coming weeks and months the reality of their loss will become stronger and it is at this time that more support may be needed. For many parents the first anniversary of their baby's death can be incredibly painful.

There are other areas of their lives too that will be emotional: the birth of new babies to friends, christenings, family occasions, the first birthdays of any children born to other couples at the same time as their little one, and watching other children grow, coupled with thoughts of how their child might have grown up and looked. Their grief is not only for the loss of their child but also for their future and their hopes and dreams.

Friends and family need to be aware of these emotional milestones in a bereaved couple's life. By making themselves available in supportive, listening roles, they can help the couple to move through their grief towards an acceptance of their loss, and to carry on with the life that had turned out differently from their original plans.

**Infant Death**

*"My baby was always happy and contented . . . she slept. I blame myself, although the hospital says it wasn't my fault, but I should have known something was wrong . . . why didn't I know? I read about other mothers who say things like they just knew. I keep thinking about her lying there, dying all alone*

*and I never comforted her. It is so painful. I hate myself. I feel so lost; my world has changed forever. I can't talk about her.*

*Sometimes I think the hospital will call me to go and get her, it's been a mistake, she's OK. I look for her in other people's prams . . . I still want to buy her things. I think other people think I did something wrong. I think I did something wrong. The emergency service came, the police came and I felt they thought I'd caused it. My husband says he knows it isn't my fault but I think he is only saying that. I go over it bit by bit, I think about everything all the time but there isn't an answer. I don't want to be with other people's babies in case something happens, and I feel envious of others too. So jealous – I think, 'Why couldn't it have happened to you?' I don't like myself for thinking that. I want to talk about it over and over, but other people tell me not to keep doing it to myself . . . they don't understand, they just think they do. This has crucified me . . . I feel so alone and empty."*

This mother believed that she had neglected her daughter, pleased to have a cup of tea before tending her child and then overwhelming guilt that she didn't check her child more closely. Thoughts flood in that if she were a 'good mother' she might have known something was wrong. Her failure for not saving or protecting her daughter. Her guilt for the times that she had left her baby crying, for the times she'd felt over tired and found mothering hard work. She was re-examining every action to try to discover what she did wrong. She needed to say all this and for it to be heard and acknowledged.

"Don't keep doing this to yourself." "Don't keep going over it." "Don't dwell on it." "It isn't your fault." "You couldn't know." Statements that are often said to those who are experiencing this trauma. It is very difficult to look and to really see, to listen and to really hear and not offer a solution, for there is no solution or easy way through the pain. Acknowledging the pain, being able and willing to hear the story time and time again without seeking to give advice or to offer consolation are not the easiest ways of helping the bereaved mother, but giving her your presence and support at this time is the most valuable and enabling assistance you can offer.

You cannot prevent a mother from blaming herself for the death of her child by telling her so. Let her acknowledge her feelings, be present while she voices her thoughts and fears again and again, so that she herself can hear them and begin, very slowly, to put them into some semblance of understanding until eventually finding her own way through these paths of pain and self-reproach.

## Sudden Accidental Death

In some instances accidental death could have been prevented. A mother called to the phone and distracted whilst her three-year-old left the garden and was subsequently hit by a vehicle and died. The parents who bought their son a motorbike on which he died. The parents who allowed their child to go on a camping trip with friends where he drowned. We have all read and heard of such incidents.

We all make decisions that, with hindsight, we know may have put our loved ones into a potentially life-threatening situation. It is the good fortune of those of us whose children survive such situations that we have the opportunity to think, "I could have lost him/her." We never think that dashing quickly to another room to get a towel whilst our babe is playing in the bath could find us attending his/her funeral in a week's time. Or that leaving our precious child playing for one moment whilst we answer the phone could provide the opportunity for him to run into the road and be killed.

This is only brought forcibly home to us either when we experience such a tragedy or when it occurs to people we know. We cannot protect our children from every danger at every moment of that child's life. All parents whose children have died in any situation blame themselves. The feelings of being unable to protect their child are overwhelming, and the guilt for not foreseeing the outcome of a decision is torturous.

> *"My son died in a house fire. It was my fault: I should have turned off those Christmas lights before leaving for my nightshift work. They looked so pretty I left them on. When I got a call in the early hours to say there had been a terrible accident at home, I knew it was my fault. I think of my son screaming in pain as he burnt . . . although my wife was there and she tried to get to him, she said he wasn't screaming, they say he died of smoke inhalation. I just can't stop hearing him. I let him down, I caused his death."*

How tempting to tell these parents it wasn't their fault and that they didn't cause the fire. We want to hush their anguished words to try to make it easier for them to bear, or for ourselves to hear. No words can ease the pain of knowing that a simple well-intentioned decision caused the loss of their child's life.

There is a need for these parents to talk about their son's death, to retell and revisit its painful experience and to face their own accusation that, if the lights had been turned off, it would not have happened. In revisiting they work through the painful and different aspects of all that happened, enabling them to say what they really think and feel without attempting to rescue, to tell and retell the story to each other and to someone who listens without judgment. They need to talk of the guilt and self-punishment and to share with each other their individual feelings. Slowly they are able to work through it, to process it, eventually accept and hopefully manage some parts of it.

> *"I always felt something would happen. He was a special child: always funny and loving and very adventurous. It's strange really, I know it sounds strange but I knew something was going to happen to him."*

Often parents tell me that they had thought about losing this child, that they had felt that something might happen and struggled to communicate to me the strong sense of something different about this child. Perhaps this child was more adventurous, more daring and caused his parents to fear they could not always protect him.

> *"He was always in trouble of some sort or another, I was always worrying about his safety. I'd shout at him to take care and he'd say, 'Yeah, yeah give it a rest.' I went to his grave and I said, 'You see – I told you. Now look what you've done.' "*

*"When the doctor told me it was a routine op I
believed him. I was a bit tearful though when she
went to theatre, I had a feeling, just a sad feeling
inside. I wish I'd said, 'No, don't do it now.' I'll
never forget the look on her beautiful little face
as they put her asleep. It's my fault. I let them
do it."*

So many parents believe that they should have known or
been able to stop their child's death. They struggle to
come to terms with and to justify the choices they made
at the time. Offering solutions or answers and trying to
give a 'feel better' factor can prevent the bereaved
parents from voicing their innermost feelings and
thoughts. These raw and anguished emotions only
multiply and fester if they are trapped within.

**The Feelings of Parents**
The word 'child' or 'children' conjures up the image of a
young person, but if you are 60, 65, 70-plus and your
parents are still alive, you are still their child! Every
parent who loses a child, no matter how old the child or
how he or she died, shares similar feelings of guilt and
failure because they did not or could not protect their
child from pain or death, or, in some cases, because they
were not present when their child died.

These are the words of many parents whose children
of different ages died.

*"The pain is so great that, when it overwhelms me,
I rock from side to side, I bang my head on the
floor and against the wall. I hit the pillow, I pinch
and punch myself, I pull my hair but it doesn't
relieve the pain I feel."*

*"I scream out to anyone, to God, space, WHY? I sob, my nose runs, my eyes swell, I want to wrap myself in sackcloth and ashes. I feel jealous, envious of others whose lives are still intact."*

*"I feel a sense of comfort when I hear of others going through this pain, though I would not wish it on my enemy. I feel guilty for feeling envious."*

*"Everything in my life is changed, everything has lost its meaning. I don't recognise my life or myself any more. I am afraid, I am afraid of my future. I long with physical pain for the past. Change disturbs me, it distresses me. The world is changing too quickly; it isn't the world my child knew. Each day something changes. I don't want change. I want things to stay the same. I don't want to move forward. Friends – no-one can understand . . . I cannot tell them, they will think I'm going crazy. In my moments of complete anguish I feel crazy."*

*"In every part of my life there is a memory. He loved beefburgers . . . I cannot bear to cook them now or to throw them out. I want to wear my pain, so that the world will bow its head as I pass, and acknowledge that my child has died."*

**The Relationship**

Often women tell me that their husbands don't talk and refuse to listen or that they feel rejected, unloved, alone and angry. Men tell me they hurt, that they are afraid to let out their 'real' feelings, that they feel a need to be strong.

There are, in my experience, huge differences in the way that men and women who experience a shared bereavement handle their emotions. It is also common for there to be marital difficulties after the death of a child. Any death can create division between couples. Where there are already difficulties, the problems may become exacerbated and, consequently, some couples can separate. Women may lose the desire for sexual intimacy, whilst men may seek comfort through closeness, but there may be guilt that they have indulged in sexual intimacy so soon after the death.

The heightened emotions and tensions within the relationship can be relieved by sexual intimacy and a release for feelings that have been contained.

*"It sounds odd but whilst we were making love I kept thinking . . . could our child see us?"*

*"I felt awful afterwards . . . how could we make love while our child lay in the chapel of rest?"*

*"Sexual contact was a release; afterwards we sobbed together . . . it was almost like we needed the release to enable us to be close enough to share our feelings."*

There are many thoughts and feelings that are too intense to share, even in the closest of relationships. Many parents don't talk openly about their grief, either with each other or outside their relationship. The feelings are so very painful and intense that they do not know where to start. They are concerned that those they tell will not be able to understand, or find the capacity to hear their pain which, to them, is too overpowering.

Between partners it is often about protection of each other and of self.

*"I don't think my husband feels like I do. He says he doesn't want to talk about it or keep going over it. He gets angry when I cry and says I have to 'get my act together'. He says that he can't stand it. He even said maybe we should separate. It feels like everything is going to pieces, I just feel so alone."*

*"What good is talking about it? It won't change anything. I am trying to survive it but it feels like I'm crucified. My wife cries all the time, she is always trying to talk about it but it scares me. If I start to talk, if I really think about it, I don't think I'll get back."*

*"Sometimes I'm just doing my work and I start crying . . . I think, 'My God it's really true', and I just feel like my insides are falling out."*

*"If I tell my husband how I really feel it will scare him. He won't be able to manage it on top of everything else and some of the things I think are just too unbearable. Also if I begin to talk about it I might not be able to manage it, it feels like it might drag me too far down and I'll never recover."*

Grief brings with it so many intense feelings: anger, despair, anxiety, guilt, hate, blame, jealousy. One woman told me that she wanted to tell other mothers how unfair it felt that they still had their child, and she wanted to shout at a mother who was smacking her child. She had anxieties about other friends, and their children aroused feelings of envy.

> *"The part of me that genuinely shared in the joy of others died with my child. I can't talk about these feelings, I'm ashamed of them but they are there. I have this hard lump in my chest. It isn't as if I can touch it, but it's there, a weight, a stone. The pain is unbearable.*
> *If anyone knew how I think they wouldn't like me . . . I don't like myself."*

The bereaved are often the protectors; they may be aware of the inability of those around them to understand and hear their pain, which often forces them to keep it locked inside them. They may think their thoughts and feelings are too shocking to voice, for fear of being judged.

> *"Why did it have to be my child? Why me? Why us? Why not ******, my sister's child? He is a handful."*

> *"Why did it have to be our son? We have three daughters . . . I wouldn't choose any of them but why wasn't it one of the girls?"*

It is not unusual for couples/parents to blame each other or to feel resentments towards each other about the death, the past, and the present, and to have little hope or thought for the future. It can feel selfish or inappropriate to grieve for loss of self or to feel anger that a relationship with a partner has changed. Old grievances and unresolved issues may rise to the surface as the parents struggle to survive whilst their world is collapsing around them.

> *"He never wanted children . . . I know secretly he's glad."*

> *"I didn't get on with our son . . . we argued most of the time. I told him I couldn't wait for him to leave home – now he's gone forever."*

> *"I blame him . . . my husband . . . he wasn't watching our child like he should have; if he had been it wouldn't have happened."*

Alongside their individual feelings and the feelings for each other within their relationship, there may be additional pressures. There may be the grief of other children to support or if their deceased child was adult there may be a partner or wife/husband and grand-children to consider.

In my experience each parent may feel like the princi-pal support mechanism. Men often don't express their feelings openly; they may try to support their female partners by trying to instil a sense of continuity or normality within the home, often by returning to work.

> *"I have to go back to work . . . I don't like the thought that others may see me going back to work and think I'm OK, that I'm over it, but if I don't go back I might lose my job and we have bills to pay. The boss has been very good, he gave me six weeks off, but I am scared that I might lose my job. Money is worrying me . . . I wish it wasn't. Sometimes I think, 'What's money now?', but I*

*have to pay the funeral costs . . . it's just so
unbearable."*

*"He was our baby, a beautiful baby, always
laughing, giggling, contented. When I went to the
hospital and saw him he looked like he was asleep.
He had that contented look. It's hard to believe he
had died so violently in that crash. I wanted to hug
him, to kiss him, to tell him I was there but I
couldn't. I felt as though it was not my place and I
felt excluded, denied my son. I felt in the way. I had
to hold on to my feelings so that we could support
his wife."*

There are many different aspects to the feelings of
ownership, not only of the deceased person, but also of
the body. This can also extend to the details of what
happened and how events unfolded. Once other people
know, the lack of privacy this causes equates to a lack
of intimacy and a lack of control.

The pain of the mother of the man who died suddenly of a heart attack was increased because she was
not able to touch her son or have her space and time
with him. She felt unable to share these feelings with
anyone as she wanted to appear supportive of her
daughter-in-law. She was concerned that others would
think her selfish or disregardful of her daughter-in-law
and of her daughter-in-law's position as next of kin to
her son. This was the beginning of resentments that,
over time, festered beneath the surface.

*"I felt like I had no rights, everyone seemed
concerned about my daughter-in-law. He was my
baby, my son, my child but because he was older I*

*was forgotten. I had to ask for information. I felt
excluded . . . so alone. When he was little and he
hurt himself I would kiss him better . . . I still felt I
wanted to kiss him better. Instead I stood by his
side – no-one said I couldn't touch him but I knew it
wasn't my place."*

It isn't unusual for parents of older children to feel
excluded. The loss of an older child can present them
with many other issues.

*"We feel guilty, we are in our seventies; he had his
life ahead of him. It should have been us first."*

*"I feel so alone now, the grandchildren don't visit us
as much either. It's as though, when our daughter
died, the whole family died with her."*

Equally, the partners of the deceased may feel that the
parents have too much involvement, and the deep feelings of exclusion and lack of ownership can create huge
breakdowns in communication.

*"They just keep telling me what I should do and
what they want. I don't want them interfering. She
was my wife."*

*"They have taken things belonging to him. I wish
they'd stop doing it but I don't want to argue with
them."*

**Regret**
In some circumstances the relationship with the child
was difficult.

*"Our daughter changed when she was 15. She became a person that we didn't know, couldn't relate to and we didn't like her much. Some nights she didn't come home and we'd go out looking for her. Our lives were so awful . . . we never knew what would happen next. She stole from us and would tell lies, all to feed her drug habit. The last time I saw her she said she hated me . . . she wished we'd just go away and leave her alone. Now she's gone . . . I feel I failed her."*

*"I had a row with my son the last time I saw him . . . I told him it would be better for us if he just stayed out of our lives . . . I wish I hadn't said that now."*

In all families there are times when there is friction between its members, where parents question their decision to marry and have a family and whether they will be able to survive the family emotional roller-coaster. Children grow, and develop, and move away from the family unit. They become influenced by the outside world and begin to develop their own thoughts, values and opinions which may be alien to those of their parents. This can be the catalyst for a breakdown in communication between parents and children. Both parents in the instances quoted have been left with a very mixed emotional response to their bereavement.

They felt guilt because they felt that they would be better off if they had never had their child. Life would be easier without the child and the problems brought to the family by the child's existence, and also because they feel relief that it is over. Those rows and disagreements will no longer occur. There will be no more worry, because what they always feared for this child has happened. But there is guilt for all that has been said in the heat of the moment, and more guilt for all the words of love and support that were left unsaid.

They felt anger that their child has finally inflicted this unending pain on them and that others may condemn them if they feel any form of relief.

*"We were always on this rollercoaster. I half expected this to happen one day . . . I feel like we finally have gone over the edge."*

*"It feels so unfair, after all the trouble we've had in the family. He was just beginning to come through it, just starting to talk to us, to be my friend. I feel I lost the opportunity to make it right between us . . . he'll never know how much I loved him."*

There is nothing that can be offered to these families except a listening ear, allowing these parents to express their feelings and their regret, anger and sadness without fear or judgment. By talking and retelling their story, they begin to make their path through their pain, face their worst thoughts and to begin to put their feelings into a more logical form. It's really not about rescuing or feeling better, it is about allowing them to survive the immediate torment of the bereavement and funeral and manage the days, weeks and months following their loss, and allowing them slowly to develop a more positive aspect on their life.

## Searching For the Child

*"I am concerned about where my child is, I know it
sounds crazy, I know she is dead, gone – and I don't
have a religious belief, I wish I did. I worry about
her being OK. I worry that she might be alone, lost
somewhere. It's all so big, too big. I mean how
could she be gone just like that?"*

The need to know that a child is all right, although the
parents know that their child is dead, may sound irrational, but is a very real and common need. They
contain this need within themselves and often will not
speak of it, which contributes to their sense of isolation
and belief that they are going crazy.

*"I noticed a black bird in the garden the other day.
It looked different from other birds. I know this
sounds ridiculous, but my son always loved the birds
in the garden . . . I was thinking could it be him?"*

The search for the child, the longing for some contact
that might confirm that he or she is still around, safe
and well is a natural need. How painful it is to accept
that someone you loved, who has been with you, that
you have held, laughed and cried with, can be gone
forever, leaving only memories. These feelings are often
expressed in the early weeks and months of bereavement, when the realisation of the permanence of the
child's absence is just too powerful. Searching for and
believing that they have seen their child is also usual in
bereaved parents.

A religious belief may offer some comfort, but for
those without a belief there may be fear about their

child's whereabouts. There may be pressure to have a belief from many, different well-meaning friends or family. "God only takes the best", "He's in heaven with Jesus" are common examples. There may be some feelings of anger with God or the parent's Supreme Being: "Why me?", "How can this be acceptable? My child belongs here with me, not with God!"

Some bereaved parents seek comfort in spiritualism or visit clairvoyants in their desperate need to know that all is well, when actually all feels far from well. Their need can also manifest itself in dreams or nightmares.

*"I see my child but, when he sees me, he runs away. I call to him, 'Please come back', but he just keeps looking over his shoulder and running . . . I wake up so anxious and sobbing."*

*"I dream that it's a mistake. I'm holding my child in my arms and telling everyone . . . look she's back . . . not dead at all. In my dream I feel such relief and then I wake up and, for a moment, I feel 'Oh, thank God it's not real', I feel so light, well relief, like a weight is lifted from me, then it's there, I realise the truth, she is dead and I feel beaten to the ground."*

It is not abnormal to experience dreams such as these, and some parents tell me that when they see their child or hold them in dreams, though it is distressing, they gain comfort. But where the child is running away or is crying or calling for the parents, the parents often say that after such traumatic dreams they feel empty.

*"I feel drained after those dreams, I feel like I've emptied my grief and for a while the feeling is manageable."*

*"I long to dream of my child, but have dreamt nothing, feel cheated that he doesn't come to me . . . give me a sign. I speak to him, I ask him just to let me know . . . but nothing."*

You cannot offer these parents comfort. You cannot offer them any hope or take away their pain. All you can do is listen or sit with them, often in silence, offering companionship in the deep, dark pit of grief.

*"I worry about the pain my child went through when she died. I wanted to ask about it but no-one would say. I know she was crying for me but I wasn't there. She died in a freak accident: a tree fell on her. I got there too late. I think about her in such pain, it's like I need to feel it with her. I feel like I let her down. I can't bear to think about her alone, lying there beneath the tree but it's all I think about."*

*"My grief comes in waves, like an ocean. Sometimes it's just still and calm. At other times it's deep, dark and so rough and the waves are so high I feel I'll drown. I never know how it is until I'm in it."*

For some parents who are present at the time of their child's death, such as at a road crash, their deep shock, trauma and hysteria can seem unmanageable to onlookers. Sometimes police or ambulance crew may remove them from the scene. In my experience this is only useful if there is an immediate danger: vehicle fire, for instance, or where the scene presents a further risk of injury. Those parents that I have worked with who were denied access to their child in those final moments are traumatised further by that denial. They are often left with overwhelming feelings of desertion and total loss of control, privacy and choice.

> *"I was there but I didn't hold my child. I was screaming at the paramedics to do something. My wife was kept back by the police. I was taken to a police car nearby. All I wanted to do was get to my little girl but they wouldn't let me. I could hear my wife screaming but they wouldn't let her near either. Even when we were at the hospital we weren't allowed to see her right away, we felt we had deserted her."*

> *"At the hospital we were not allowed to touch our child, he was kept in a room I think. My husband identified him but we only saw him through a window. It was so awful. We wanted to hold him, to love him, to let him know we were there but they said we couldn't do that yet. We felt that he belonged to them."*

The feeling that their child was taken from the parents not only by death but by those in official roles is common. Parents frequently tell me that they felt they couldn't ask what happened, or that touching or moving their dead child was not permitted and that in some way their child was no longer theirs. They feared that their desire to be with their child might be viewed as strange or morbid.

*"Our daughter in her coffin looked so different lying flat like that. I hadn't seen her like that before. I remember thinking about Sleeping Beauty; yes, that's how she looked. She had bandages on her arms. I wanted to look at her arms to see why but I felt them watching me so I didn't touch her. I kissed her forehead but even that felt intrusive. I wanted to take her nose piercing for myself but I was scared to touch her and scared to ask the funeral director in case he said no. I didn't tell my husband either. I didn't tell anyone how I just wanted to pick up her broken body and hug her and bring her home."*

*"I went to see our boy every day at the funeral home. It made it easier that we could still see him although he looked different. I wish we could have brought him home but I didn't think they'd let us."*

I cannot tell you how many times parents have said these things to me. Why can we not ask the bereaved what they want? What do we think they are going to do with the body? Secrete it away somewhere, never parting with it? Parting is painful and distressing but by being given space, privacy and time to spend in private goodbyes the parting is made more manageable.

## Unspoken Thoughts

*"I worry about my child's body. I think about it under the ground, especially when it's wet. I wanted to ask someone how long it would take before it decomposed, but I think they'll think I'm morbid."*

*"I worry about my child being safe in his grave. I don't like it that he is so far away. I wish I could have buried him in my garden."*

*"I try to go to the grave every day. Once a dog ran over my daughter's grave and I felt so angry with the owner: I felt my child had been disregarded."*

*"I put balloons and teddies on my child's grave but someone took them."*

*"I feel like our child is alone in the cemetery. I wanted to keep the ashes at home but my husband said it would distress visitors."*

*"I went to get my child's ashes. There didn't seem to be enough. I've read that sometimes you don't get the right ones but I was scared to ask anything."*

*"My child was cremated. I don't know what happened. I'd like to know."*

*"I didn't see my child. He drowned and the funeral director said it might be better not to see him. I wanted to but I was afraid and I felt the funeral director might insist."*

*"My daughter's body was never found. I sometimes think when I'm driving – is she there? I am always searching."*

*"It's like being in a pool. Sometimes I am staying afloat but mostly I feel I'm drowning."*

*"My child was in the hospital. They did an autopsy.
I saw he had a cut by his throat. I wanted to know
what they had done to him. No-one told me and my
husband said it would only distress us more. What
could distress us more?"*

What could distress these parents more than the
unknown? Often the unknown is more frightening, more painful than the reality. If they don't ask,
don't tell. If they don't ask, does it mean that they
don't want to know? Is it our fear of upsetting the
parents or are we worried about our own inability to
communicate?

In some circumstances the death may be reported by
the media, in the press and on TV. When this happens
lack of privacy and intrusion are often felt and parents
can feel that they have lost their child to the general
public and that their grieving has to be done under the
public's gaze.

*"All those things written about us. Details about
our child's death were written for everyone to read.
It feels like people know all about us – people who
we don't even know. We aren't private any more. I
think about them: they're not really bothered or
able to understand how it is for us, like we were
before. They probably think, 'Oh, how awful, poor
people.' It always happens to others, stuff like this –
we are the others now."*

*"It feels like they have some ownership on us, and
everything they know about it feels like a piece of it
is taken from us. It's like we have nothing left that
is ours and ours alone."*

When a child has died traumatically, in an accident or has been the victim of murder, details may be revealed to the press. Alongside the information given by police there will be added information about the family, the child's life or the story behind the child's death.

Families often find this intrusion difficult to manage and many are further distressed by reports and concerned about the reactions of those who may know them. There is little that can be done about reports and information made public but a great deal can be achieved by forward planning and talking through possible reports and reactions, thus aiding the manageability of situations and the avoidance of additional trauma.

**Your Child's Room**

I say much in this book about the individuality of grief and the diversity of feelings experienced by each and every person. I have also acknowledged that males and females grieve differently, quite apart from cultural, religious and genetic backgrounds.

Alongside the differences of gender is each parent's individual relationship with the child. This can often be the cause of added stress and misunderstandings, resentments, blame and anxieties.

*"After our daughter died I used to sit in her room*
*for hours, just breathing in the smell of her.*
*Sometimes I'd take her clothes from the cupboard*
*and bury my face in them just to get a sense of her,*
*a familiar piece of the reality . . . yes, she was here.*
*I sometimes got into her bed too and that is where I*
*did a lot of my crying. I always waited until I was*
*alone in the house then I'd give myself permission*
*to go to pieces. I couldn't bear the thought of*

*anyone moving her things or taking them. I'm so grateful that my husband didn't try to stop me, although a friend expressed concerns about my behaviour, she couldn't understand. It wasn't about shrine building, it was about accepting and letting go of her slowly in my own way. It was five years before I felt able to begin to change her room and ready to put her things away."*

*"I came home from shopping and found boxes outside the door: my husband and parents had cleared our child's room whilst I was out. I was devastated. I couldn't believe that they would do that. Did they think that if they stripped his room I'd be better?"*

*"I felt this need to pack up my son's things when we came back from hospital after he'd died. My husband sat there in his room on his bed. I washed his clothes and ironed them. It was as though I needed to do it although I knew he'd never wear them again. I put some things in bags under the stairs. I can't bear to look at them. I don't know when I'll move the rest of his things – is there a time-limit?"*

*"My son committed suicide in his room. The police went into everything; it felt so intrusive. We have just left it like that for now. People keep offering to sort it out for us but we aren't ready to do it yet."*

For some parents the room was not the focus of their grief, while for others the room was a significant place, where they felt their grief was permitted. Some put their child's possessions away quickly and sometimes that's all right. Others find comfort in surrounding themselves with the room and belongings of their child, taking comfort and releasing their grief in the smell and feel of the child around them. Some close the door and cannot bring themselves to cross the threshold. Change is not easy to manage and a task such as changing the bedding or washing the clothes can be overwhelmingly painful.

*"Two weeks after my daughter's funeral I was at home alone and decided to go to her room. I began to tidy up. I was OK, a bit tearful, but managing it until I took the sheets off her bed. As I put them into the washing machine I thought, 'That's the last time she'll ever sleep in those sheets.' It felt like I was washing her away."*

Is there a right way to be? In the early days it is, I believe, a case of getting by in whichever way you can. By the minute, by the hour if that is what it takes. It's allowed to close the door on your child's bedroom, leaving it just as it is so you can spend time in the room in the early days. It is also important to recognise the choices of other family members. If the room was shared, for instance, it is important to ask the sharer(s) how they might like to see the room change or stay the same. Some families decide to change the use of the room to something else. Again, time, space and consideration for all involved is essential. Decorating the room can be as hard as changing the bed linen or packing up toys and belongings. Physically changing something from the way it was is a final confirmation that the child will not be returning to the bedroom. Some parents feel they are deserting their dead child by getting on with their lives.

*"It was almost a year before we decorated the room; it was incredibly hard. We felt like we were leaving part of him behind, moving on, removing him. Our daughter has the room now, but it's hard not to keep calling it John's room."*

When people ask me about change, when and how to do it, I suggest that they think about what they want to change. It is all about giving yourself permission to do something your way. If it feels too hard, leave it. Maybe it is not the right time yet. There are no hard and fast rules that say you must clear out the belongings and make changes until you feel able to do so. It will never be easy but in time it becomes more manageable. Keeping memory boards, a journal or memory box with a few favourite items is a way of keeping memories together and easily accessible and can be useful in enabling you to progress through the grieving process.

Sometimes, in the early days, it can be tempting to want to give others a memento of your child. Of course you can do this, but usually it's better to wait a short while as it can feel right to give something away one day, but, the next day, you wish you hadn't done so.

## Moving On?

*"I am finding even small changes hard to live with. It feels as each day goes by that something changes and the world as my son knew it has changed so much, even in a few months. You don't notice change normally but now I feel like I'm moving on from him."*

It can be incredibly difficult to express and manage the feelings that can be evoked by change.

*"It may sound crazy but I don't want to cut the grass. I know my daughter stood on that grass and it feels like there's this blackboard with her life on it and slowly it's being wiped out."*

These are not crazy thoughts. They are thoughts that may not have been expressed in the open. But they have been felt, thought and feared in the mind, and in isolation, in some degree by each and every bereaved person with whom I have worked, or who has contacted me.

Bereaved parents are also very conscious about what people on the outside think of them.

*"Do they think we are OK . . . over it . . . moving on?"*

*"If we go out, do they think, 'Ah . . . life's back to normal now?' "*

*"We had to get a new car after the crash. A neighbour saw us out and said, 'Oh, lovely car . . . did you win the lottery?' Before I could answer, he said, 'Nice to see you getting better.' I know he didn't think about any of his words, but it caused me so much distress, anger and frustration. Actually no-one understands how we really are."*

*"We have new neighbours. They'll never know our child. I want to put a huge photo outside saying 'I used to live here.' "*

The diversity of feelings experienced by the bereaved is complicated. On the one hand, the bereaved want the world to acknowledge the loss of their child and their grief. On the other, they resent the intrusions into their privacy. They feel anger that those who have no real understanding of the depth of their grief perhaps offer words of comfort in what may feel hurtful or inappropriate ways.

> *"I was doing the garden when a neighbour came over. I felt very anxious, like my chest was getting so tight. She said, 'I'm so sorry to hear about your little one'; I said, 'Thank you.' All the time my chest was tightening like a fist was there squeezing it. I said something about the weather, she said it was nice to see me out and getting on. Then she said, 'You have other children, don't you?' and I said, 'Yes,' and she said, 'Oh well then, they'll keep you busy.' It's not the first time that I've felt like it's OK because, after all, I've got my other children."*

The hurt was not intentional but said by way of offering something positive. As a society our reaction when faced with someone who has been recently bereaved is to bring out the 'doing well' blanket, to offer our condolences alongside some promise of brighter days, so reassuring the bereaved that they will get over it. Are we really reassuring ourselves? Bereavement cannot be got over easily but in time it may become, on some days, a little easier to live with. However, the acknowledgement, that the death has changed things permanently, may just be too incomprehensible and uncomfortable for those less involved to accept. For each and every one of us, there is always the possibility that, in one moment, some tragic event could impact on our life and steal away our children, leaving devastation in its wake, and causing unforeseen and unimaginable changes.

The most immediate change is to the family, their members' relationship with each other and with the outside world. This reality is often felt but undisclosed by the bereaved. Why? Our society has no time for circumstances that cannot be healed or cured, not even by the passage of time. It makes all of us feel vulnerable, exposed and out of control. What is the old saying? What cannot be cured must be endured. That is what we expect the bereaved parents to do: to endure their loss and grief, preferably in privacy and out of our sight, so we do not have to suffer alongside them and face the reality of mortality.

### Family Dynamics

When a child dies, the dynamics within the family are changed. A child who was once an elder or younger sibling may now be an only child and children who have lost an only sister or brother now become the 'only' boy or the 'only' girl.

Parents who lose a child can transfer their understandable anxieties to the children they still have, trying to offer those children the protection and love they may feel they did not give the child who died.

*"We were a very laid back family, relaxed. Now I feel anxious all the time and I don't like the children to be away too long or to go out alone. I know it's hard on them but I'm scared something might happen."*

The feelings of loss of control, the anxieties caused by the upheaval to what was once a secure and stable family relationship, are overwhelming. The effect on the family can be extremely destructive as everyone tries to manage their own grief and still present a positive outer image for the other members of the family. Parents often feel the need to keep their remaining children close to them. Those children may, in turn, feel resentful of this new and restrictive regime and lack of freedom. There may be arguments and outbursts of anger, the like of which were never previously experienced. Disagreements and pressure from other family members can cause additional anxieties to the grieving parents and these in turn can contribute to a breakdown in the relationship and their ability to communicate with each other.

Parents may feel responsible for the death or may blame each other or other family members. There may be feelings of animosity towards older family members, who are still alive, when the younger member has died.

*"I feel angry with my husband's mother. She has all these health problems. If anyone should be dead it should be her. Now she is even worse. I feel angry that she is using our son's death to get more attention."*

It is not unusual for feelings like these to be present, or for previous grievances unconnected to the death to become magnified, and become the focus of the emotional impact of the death. Grandparents' health is often greatly affected by the trauma caused by the death of a grandchild. It can create many issues for them – not least that the perceived order of things has been changed (the younger dying before the elder), and they may find themselves feeling guilty for living. Where once a family may have been sympathetic to the older person's ailments, now these may be triggers for feelings of deep resentment.

*"My mother was always complaining of this pain or that pain and it used to cause problems because I felt that I ought to give her lots of consideration; we were very close. My husband said that she was an attention seeker. Many of her ailments began when my father died ten years ago. I felt sorry for her. The children used to get irritated as sometimes plans had to be changed to facilitate my mother's needs. Then last year she was diagnosed with terminal cancer. I devoted so much time to her care and I resented my family for not being more generous. If I had not been at my mother's that day, our daughter wouldn't have been driven by her friend and wouldn't have died. Now I can't feel the same about my mother. I resent her for being here and, you know, I also resent that she is going to die soon and escape this agony. My husband and I hardly speak; he blames me for our daughter's death, I blame myself. My mother says, 'It should've been me. I want to die.' I think she feels guilty but I feel so angry when she says that too, because she is going to die and will be with my daughter. I feel I've lost my daughter, my family, my mother and myself. I don't know what to do any more. Our son has left home. No-one seems to understand, my husband is so distant. What's life about?"*

For this mother all relationships within her family were changed by the sudden death of her daughter in a car crash. The impact of her daughter's death has changed everything. She suffers feelings of resentment towards her mother, guilt for feeling that resentment, coupled with guilt for feeling responsible for her daughter's death; she feels anger and distress at her loss of relationship with both husband and remaining child.

> *"I blame my son for the death of my grandchildren; he was too laid back, he allowed them to do anything they wanted, he wouldn't listen. Yes, I blame him and I want him to know but I can't say it. I don't visit much and I know they are finding it hard to be together. I think my daughter-in-law blames him too."*

Disconnecting from the family isn't unusual. Often after the death the extended family find their feelings so overwhelming that they choose to have less contact while they come to terms with these emotions, but this can add to the isolation felt by the grieving family.

> *"I can't talk to my husband about how I'm feeling. He keeps saying we have to move on, but I'm not ready. He goes to church and takes our other son but I can't go there. I hate God for this."*

Everyone manages their unique experience of grief differently:

> *"My mum doesn't want to go out or do anything with me. I feel like saying, 'My sister's dead but I'm alive!'"*

*"My parents are separating. I hate my brother.
Even in death he is the cause of family problems.
When is it going to end?"*

*"This is too painful. I wish I'd never had children,
stayed on my own. I want to leave my wife and get
away from this."*

*"We can't communicate. Every time we try to talk
we end up arguing, then crying and it feels like
everything is falling apart."*

If the family are to survive this together it is essential
that they communicate and that every member of the
family has the opportunity to talk as much or as little as
they feel able. Parents need to share their grief and not
attempt to conceal it in order to protect the remaining
children. Everyone in the family needs to feel able to
voice the feelings, thoughts and fears they hold inside
themselves, even the youngest children. They are often
forgotten, or feel they must be strong, because that is
what 'grown ups' do.

### The Death of a Sibling
The death of a brother or sister will affect the remaining
brothers or sisters differently according to their age and
their understanding of death. Circumstances play a
large part in how the remaining sibling or siblings come
to accept the death. For example, a child who has a long
history of terminal illness will have had a particular
relationship with his or her siblings who may, from a
very early age, have been exposed to the reality that this
child may not live a long life. Sudden accidental death,
because of its unexpected nature, will have a different

effect on siblings. There are, however, similarities in the needs of all bereaved children: the need to talk and for people to listen to them.

> *"My brother Tom was playing in the road and he was run over by a car and he died. I don't think people can come back when they die. It's scary, I don't want to die."*

Children are often left with fantasy about death. Much of the information they already have comes from films or television in which the nature and permanency of death is glossed over. Parents are naturally consumed by their grief for their deceased child and it is not unusual for the living children to become their defenders, protectors of their parents. Indeed sometimes this task is conferred on them by well-meaning relatives or friends.

> *"Don't let Mummy or Daddy see you cry. You must be brave/be good/be strong."*

Statements such as these are offered in the belief that they are helpful, but the pressures on siblings can be overwhelming: the pressure to be good, to be strong, to get on with life and, in some cases, to be perfect in the absence of the sibling. There may be guilt for living when their brother or sister is dead, or self-blame, and often anger or jealousy.

There may be fear about death, especially when remaining siblings are at a very young age when their understanding of the finality of death is limited. They may fear that, like their sibling, they too may die. Where families have religious or cultural beliefs, these, alongside other stories, may be offered to the remaining children as comfort.

*"Tom has gone to be a bright star for Jesus."*

*"I don't want Tom to be a star . . . I was a good boy too and I want to be a star."*

*"I don't want Tom to be a star because he will be lonely and I can't play with him now."*

Some well-meaning, comforting platitudes said to surviving small children may be misconstrued as rejection. Parents may tell them that their dead sibling was extra special and chosen to be an angel. Most of us have heard the statement 'The good die young'. Do they? Does this mean that we who grow old are bad? Of course not. But the horror of death, particularly the death of a child, leaves all of us looking for a reason why. The reality is not easy to accept and the change in the perceived order of life can cause great insecurities for both young and old alike. Reality, unlike fantasy, has an end. Fantasy can become unmanageable and is governed only by the limitations of one's mind.

Small children are often left without support. Their ability to communicate may be limited by their experience, age and understanding. It is important that even the very young are invited to talk about their feelings and to share their thoughts about death and dying with someone who will listen and accept all their words.

It is sad that a young child's life may be affected by death. Childhood is seen as a time of innocence and naivety, and the loss of both of these seemingly desirable experiences early on is upsetting. But it can create experiential growth. Death need not always be destructive. Children have the ability to dip in and out of emotion, one moment immersed in grief, the next playing happily. It is important that questions are answered when asked, and that they be answered honestly, but taking into account the child's ability to comprehend the answer.

> *"When our son Tom died he was 11, our younger son, Joe, was 6. We let Joe go and stay with his grandparents, we were so shocked and Joe didn't understand, not really. I remember being really angry with Joe because on the way back from the funeral directors we passed a fairground. Joe said, 'Oh look Mummy, a fair. After Tom's funeral can we go?' I was so angry. It was as though he didn't understand, and, of course, he didn't, but we somehow thought he would."*

Even though Joe had been told about his brother's death, it didn't mean that he understood. He appeared to be aware of all that was happening, he was present when they talked to the police and he saw how distressed his parents and other family members were. He knew that Tom wasn't there and was aware of a sense of deep sadness around. The house, although busy with unusual amounts of visitors, had a different feel to it. He was aware of having more attention but unable to make sense of it all.

He became scared at night when he was alone and afraid that others might leave him. He thought that it might be his fault and he looked for Tom wherever he went. Joe's parents found dealing with his emotional needs, whilst going through their own grief, incredibly difficult. In such circumstances, external support is invaluable and a place where Joe could talk openly and explore his feelings and thoughts would benefit both Joe and his parents.

When Frank (23) died in a freak accident at work his sister Joanne (15) was devastated:

*"I was 15 when Frank died. I remember coming home from school and there being a lot of cars outside the house. I just knew something was wrong. Everyone was there: my uncles, aunts and grandparents. I went into the house and my aunt said, 'It's Frank. He's had an accident at work, he's dead.' I was really shocked. I shouted for Mum but they wouldn't let me in the front room. My uncle said I could go with him to the shop to get tea and milk and stuff. I was just shocked. I can't remember much, but going into the shop I told someone and it felt unreal. I didn't talk much to Mum or Dad. I tried to make tea for them and they just sat there staring. No-one really asked if I was OK. I cried so much, but only when I was alone. I sat in Frank's room too, and I begged him to come and for it to be a dream. Our house was so busy. I wanted people to go away but they kept coming round. I didn't go to school but I can't remember what I did. I wore his tee shirt. Mum and Dad went to see him at the funeral directors. I said I didn't want to go, and now I wish I had because I felt like I let him down. At the funeral I was with Mum and Dad but I felt alone and I really needed Frank to be there; he always looked after me.*

*Things have changed so much at home, Mum said she wants to just die. I feel that sometimes, but other times I feel angry that Frank died and our life has changed. Sometimes I want to shout, 'Frank's dead but I'm still here!' Recently I have felt angry with him for causing all this. It's not fair."*

Joanne was largely forgotten amidst the grief and shock of Frank's death. Quite quickly she began to fit into the role of carer to the family and her own grief became contained inside herself, but, mixed with her feelings of loss and of deep sadness, were resentment, anger and, in turn, guilt. Over a period of time she became depressed due to the lack of opportunity to release these pent-up emotions which bubbled and fermented inside her.

Martina was 11 when her twin sister drowned whilst on holiday. Martina was swimming with her sister, Natalia, but could not save her.

*"I don't remember what happened but I think it was my fault, I should have saved her. I think it should have been me who drowned because Natalia was a better swimmer. I sometimes think that other people, like the family, think it should have been me too, because she was a special person."*

It is not unusual for children to feel responsible, less important or devalued following the death of a sibling. They may believe their sibling to be far more special or more loved than themselves because grieving and shocked parents often make casual comments declaring how special, gifted and beautiful the deceased sibling was, unaware of the vulnerability and feelings of inadequacy these can cause in the living children.

This feeling that the deceased sibling has been elevated to an unattainable position, and is forever being compared with them, can begin to grow even in very young children, who may be told by mourning parents how wonderful their sister or brother was.

In some cases, parents may decide to have more children.

> *"I never knew my sister, she died two years before I was born, in a road accident. I have always felt like the family compare me or look for her in me. This sounds silly, but it's true. Once I did something and my aunt said that I did it in just the same way as my sister. I have felt like I've had almost to be someone I don't know."*

Children who are left to face life without their siblings need a great deal of support in safely exploring both positive and negative feelings that are usual in such circumstances. They need reassurance that they too are worthwhile people in their own right, that they are loved for themselves, and that they are important to their parents. They need to have these points emphasised to them time and time again, not just in the period of time after their siblings' death but as they mature. Hopefully, they will slowly start to believe that they too have a value as a member of the family and are not just a poor substitute for their dead brother or sister.

# 5

# SUDDEN, VIOLENT OR TRAUMATIC DEATH

This chapter is written for those of you whose loved ones have died in traumatic circumstances, either in an accident, or through suicide, acts of violence or as victims of terrorist attack or murder.

The experience of a sudden or unexpected death impacts in a very different way from that of expected death, where there may be some degree of emotional or mental preparation.

In Chapter 1 I wrote about the reactions to news of sudden death: the shock and devastation and the numbness. In this chapter I hope to expand on and contribute to a greater understanding of this trauma. I seek to assist those of you who want to support the bereaved through their grief. Hopefully you can reassure those who have been bereaved that they are not going mad or losing their mind. Bizarre and irrational thoughts at this time are usual and many people in the same situation feel like that.

The story of the death . . . What happened?. . . How did it happen?. . . Where did it happen?. . . How much suffering was caused or experienced by the loved one?

These are the main areas that the families of those who died a sudden death will explore, often in isolation. In those lonely hours when lying awake during the night they try to piece together parts of all that has happened and those parts that they cannot quite remember or recall. There are often fantasies about the loved one's death and the added fantasy of the loved one surviving.

*"I often think about my husband's last moments. I try not to but I can't get my mind away from it. Sometimes he is calling for me, he is in need and I'm not there. Sometimes I work at trying to put myself there with him and I fantasise about all of the things I'd do to help him. Sometimes I fantasise that I rescue him. I dream about him calling me too. The reality is he died alone on a roadside, and though they say they think his death was instant, I know he must have felt something, had thoughts and it tortures me."*

It is normal to need to keep going over the details. Many people have told me that they find it difficult to talk about their thoughts and feelings for several reasons: they don't want to be a nuisance; the things they want to say are too horrific; others may think they are losing their minds; they think that they ought to be getting on with or over it and often, most importantly, they need to protect their remaining loved ones.

Where the death has been caused by disaster, or terrorist attack, or where there are several deaths of unrelated persons at the same time, the bereaved are carried along on a wave of public attention, the camaraderie of group and the organised care which in the immediate aftermath provide support and comfort.

However, at this time the families are in shock and operating by automatic function. They may seem fully involved and participating, but it is afterwards that the sense of belonging fades. The group disperses and they go to their separate homes and to reality. Then their real feelings start to emerge. These emotions can be diverse, changing direction from one moment to the next.

> *"There was a nurse who was just so amazing. She listened and I was able to talk and talk. Sometimes I feel nothing but gratitude towards her. Then this other feeling emerges, I feel angry that she was there, that I shared my stuff so willingly. Though I can remember her face, I will do forever, I can't remember everything I said. So now I feel like she knows my stuff. I don't like to feel angry with those who help but sometimes I do."*

> *"I regret talking to the press. I feel like it's not my story any more. It's everyone's – strangers know things about me. To them I'm just news."*

The vulnerability of the bereaved and of those who are in trauma and shock is frequently exploited. They have a deep need, a driving force to keep telling the story of what happened over and over again in an attempt to make sense of it, to work it through, to put it together, to get the whole picture. This exposure can leave them with overwhelming feelings of exploitation and lack of ownership of the story of their loved one's death.

> *"I feel cheated that my husband is a number. I feel cheated that his death is part of a huge death; it's lost amidst the event. Does this sound selfish? In*

*some ways I gain comfort from other families – they
know how it is. But sometimes I just want to stand
up and shout his name and tell the world this is who
died."*

*"The difference is the world will go on, they talk in
public speeches about bravery, they call my husband
a hero. I feel angry that it's all so public, and that
they will move on. But I can't. Things will never
ever be the same."*

The observation by the public of death through disaster
or human act, the leaving of flowers, sending of cards
and letters, the grouping and get-togethers is short-
lived. In a few months, all the bereaved families are left
with is the reality of life without their loved one and
maybe even the feeling of being forgotten by the people
who had surrounded and seemed to care about them
only a short while ago.

In some circumstances the family may be present at
the moment of death. The trauma of observing or being
part of the horror can cause them further distress.
Surviving a crash or event where others, including loved
ones, have died can be the cause of tremendous guilt,
helplessness and self-blame. Perhaps members of the
family were present but were restrained by emergency
services or medical staff from being with their loved
ones in their final moments. In months to come the
memory of this can add to their mental torment.

*"I was at the scene but the police wouldn't let me
near. I could see my daughter's legs and her bike.
At one point I am certain I heard her call out
'Mummy' but the police officer was holding me*

*back. I remember pleading to be allowed to go to her but they took me in a police car behind the ambulance. When we arrived at the hospital they took me to a room, I kept asking about my daughter. It seemed like ages. When my husband arrived they told us she had died. I wanted to know where, when, but the time on the death certificate indicates she died in hospital. Why wasn't I with her? I think she died at the roadside. I feel I let her down. I know she called me. It haunts me. Now I feel so angry with them for denying me being with her."*

There may be many reasons why family are not allowed immediate access to their loved one. Sometimes the reasons are practical or there are safety or legal reasons, for example, it is the scene of a crime, but sometimes it may be deemed by the 'professionals' involved to be just too distressing for the family to witness.

In Chapter 1 I wrote about the importance of offering the family choices, keeping information truthful, and offering it without drama or effect. The bereaved are initially in a state of shock. Such considerations as using simple words wherever possible, avoiding medical or legal jargon, writing down information and offering the bereaved an opportunity to request information as they wish – all these are ways of helping them to absorb the circumstances of their loved one's death. People tell me that they were given information verbally but cannot recall it and didn't like to keep asking for parts of it to be repeated as they didn't want to be a nuisance.

In certain circumstances the body may be held as evidence and may not be released to the family for several days. Families may find official procedures bewildering, restricting and confusing. Professionals used to such circumstances may unwittingly neglect to pass on small details or pieces of information. The importance of the Police Liaison Officer's input at this time cannot be too strongly emphasized; his/her relationship with the family can greatly influence their management of the tragedy.

**Suicide**

*"Every day I wake up asking myself the same question – WHY?"*

Families and loved ones of those who choose to end their own lives are all faced with the unanswerable question – why? Even those families where the deceased may have left notes, or attempted suicide before, find it hard to understand why someone they loved took his or her own life. Suicide may be felt by those left behind as a reflection on them, a sign of their failure to keep the loved one alive and their failure to help, and, most hurtful of all, a feeling of rejection by their loved one.

Suicide is sometimes committed with no obvious reason or prior warning and comes as a complete shock to the family/loved ones. On other occasions the threat has been present for a while, or there has been depression and previous attempts before the act has finally succeeded.

*"Our son was ill for quite a few years; he was suffering depression and was receiving medication. Recently he had been receiving treatment that seemed to be doing him some good and we felt*

*that he just might be getting better. On the morning of his death he phoned me and he sounded very chirpy. He said he was looking forward to coming home at the weekend. It was a total shock when the police came and told us that he had taken his life. He had hanged himself. I feel like I failed him, I should have known he was going to do it. I am tortured by the thought that he died alone, that he must have been so much more depressed, more unhappy than we knew. I feel physical pain that my son went through it alone. I will never forgive myself."*

Many children and adults contemplate suicide at some time in their lives. Those that consider it do not always follow it through. In my experience there are no set patterns. The reasons are many: a broken relationship, low self-esteem, loneliness and no-one to tell, the sense of despair in the lonely hours, feeling that life is never going to be how you want it to be, unable to see an alternative, life seeming bleak, a future too frightening to face, a call for help where actions can speak louder than any words.

"If they know I want to die because of this, they'll take notice. They'll be sorry when I'm gone!"

Those who commit suicide perhaps need confirmation that they have value and are important to someone. Irrationally they believe that this will be acknowledged once they are dead; irrational because, of course, they will not be there to experience or acknowledge it.

Suicide may feel like the only option for teens who believe they are ugly or whose acne has caused them to feel life is not worth living. Children who are bullied may be seeking release from their tormenters. Those who fear failure or believe that they are never going to achieve anything good in life may seek escape.

*"My daughter was a happy girl, never a problem, always funny and lively until she became the victim of a group at school who, over a period of time, destroyed her self-esteem with their comments, verbal abuse and bullying.*

*She became introverted and refused to go anywhere without us. She said she would be better off dead – I never for one moment thought those words were so seriously felt. I said something like, 'Don't be silly. This is a phase. They are jealous of you.' I said all those things that I felt were true, helpful and encouraging. Sometimes I got angry with her. Just before she died I went to her room and said, 'Is this it then? Are you going to let those girls win? Stay in your room and never go out?' I shouted at her to pull herself together.*

*When I got back from a shopping trip the house was quiet and I thought, 'Thank goodness, she's gone out.' I even thought perhaps my shouting had done it, finally made her get it together.*

*I didn't go to her room until supper time. I went to put her laundry away and I couldn't open the door. She had pushed her bed against the door and, earlier that day, maybe not long after my shouting, she hanged herself. She didn't leave a note."*

On reflection, this mother felt she had failed her daughter: why hadn't she recognised the depth of her daughter's despair and why hadn't she known how serious it was?

She suffered the torments of 'should haves', 'would

haves' and 'could haves'. Had she failed her child? Have we as a society failed those who choose to end their lives?

Perhaps with the benefit of hindsight it is easier to see how we could have reacted differently, but I have no doubt that a person who is seriously intent on suicide will eventually succeed. So where does this leave those who are left to manage life without their loved one? Unlike other types of death it leaves most with overwhelming feelings of guilt, failure and unanswered and unanswerable questions. Asked by anyone how their loved one died there is often added anxiety of how the truth may be received. The word 'suicide' is an unforgiving word; the very mention of it instantly causes the enquirer discomfiture, the fear of probing further and raises unsaid and unspoken thoughts. The bereaved know or think they know those thoughts. Is suicide a statement about or a reflection on the family of the victim? Does a person's choice to die reflect the family's failure to help him or her through the trauma he or she experienced and ultimately was unable to face? What is the stigma – my child committed suicide, did I fail him/her?

We can only work within our experience of the present, this moment in time. The mother whose child hanged herself because of bullying hadn't failed her child at all. She had practised her parenting skills to the best of her ability; she had listened, talked, encouraged and tried to boost her child.

*"My ex-partner threatened to kill himself several times and there were two attempts. The first time I raced up the motorway to be with him. He had overdosed but called paramedics himself. Afterwards we got back together and things did improve but deep down I knew I'd only got back with him*

*because I felt responsible. I began to feel very depressed and, after a visit to my GP, was on medication. I became more down, he became aggressive and at that point I wanted to leave. He said if I left he'd kill us both and on one occasion he tried to drive the car off the road. After this I left him. I was called at work; they said he'd tried to cut his wrists. Again I went to see him. I felt so guilty because this time I wished he'd died. I tried to keep friends with him but he seemed unpredictable, sometimes rational and accepting of our separation and of friendship, at others he'd threaten me or talk of ways he could kill himself. I was so depressed by it all that I had to give up work; my life was collapsing. I felt trapped by him. There was no escape. Every night I'd pray he would do it. Then he did. He took an overdose and drowned himself. At first I was so relieved and glad, a weight lifted, but now I feel responsible, guilty and I'm tormented by thoughts about it and a note he left saying he didn't want to live without me and he was sorry. To be honest I feel relieved but I don't like myself for feeling it and I know those who know him blame me."*

For some people, the relief of no longer living with the threat of another person's suicide is enormous. These feelings, mixed with grief for loss of the person, are complicated, confusing, difficult to talk about and express.

*"My daughter was a cutter, she began self-harm about five years ago at around 13 years old. I took her to see so many specialists. Sometimes it felt like things were better but then it would go downhill*

*again. It was like riding an emotional rollercoaster.
Our family lived on the edge, never knowing what
would happen next. I tried so hard to keep her
going but she seemed unreachable. The last six
months of her life were hell for all of us and when
she took her life I felt thank God it's over. I
remember standing by her coffin at the chapel of
rest and looking at her: she looked peaceful at last.
I miss her so much, it's incredibly painful but I am
relieved that for all of us it's over. It's so isolating
to feel relief and grief together."*

In my experience, the separation of the positive and
negative aspects of life and death for those living on
after suicide need to be expressed and accepted. I
wrote in Chapter 1 about our need when talking
with the bereaved to make better, to offer positive
thoughts and words and to disregard the negative. It
is tempting to tell the bereaved loved ones of a
suicide that they are not to blame, and to hush their
words with kind and soothing remarks and actions.
But, in my experience, this serves only to push
inwards their unspoken words and thoughts, and
isolate them further.

*"I feel, I know I am to blame. I know everyone
thinks I could have done more, although they don't
say it. I sometimes feel I want to wear a board
saying, 'My partner killed herself – it's my fault',
that's what I think they are thinking."*

*"Some days I feel so angry with her for doing this.
I think she was selfish. We needed her. How could
our mother not want to live for us?"*

*"My partner was diagnosed with terminal illness;
she was afraid of dying slowly and I know this was
her way of controlling it. I know she didn't want us
to suffer it with her. I feel she did it for us. I
understand it, but I wish she had shared it with us. I
wish we had known how she felt. I think about her
dying alone and it tortures me."*

*"I feel so very ashamed; I can't grieve my son's
death because in choosing to kill himself he killed
an innocent driver too. I cannot allow myself to
grieve for him. I miss him so much. Why did he do
this? Why didn't he tell me? Why didn't he talk to
me? I could have helped him. I would have been
there more. I should have known. Why?"*

*"I am haunted by his last moments. How much did
he suffer? When I think about it – oh my God it's
torture!"*

Suicide, death by choice, has so many stigmas attached
to it. It is the combination of these stigmas and the
sense of being judged that makes the bereaved feel
isolated. There is fear of being labelled and being the
focus of misinformed and often cruel and judgmental
gossip. The pain felt by the bereaved and their grief,
alongside those unanswered questions, can be overwhelming. Sometimes the belief that they are to blame,
and the overwhelming guilt because of this, becomes
almost too much to bear. Did he/she really mean to do
this? Could it have been a mistake?

*"I don't know whether I believe in God but it
troubles me because someone said that suicide is a*

*crime in God's eyes and suicides cannot be buried in consecrated ground. The minister at our church was very kind and supportive but I worry about my child. It sounds bizarre to say that because I don't know if there is a God or not."*

*"Someone said that it was disgusting that my husband killed himself. I feel so ashamed. I don't want people to know."*

Sadly suicide is so often seen as a reflection on a family and their life together, and this can add to the stigma. Most coroners are cautious to record death by suicide. Families are often fearful of such public statement. They think that, if the cause of death is publicly recorded as suicide, then they will have to live with the unanswered questions and uncertainty forever.

However, once a death is recorded as suicide the families are left with no alternative but to face the truth. There is no more of the grey area where it can be said that their loved one died by 'accident'. The desire for death and rejection of life stares everyone brutally in the face and brings with it, in so many cases, the suspicion of personal rejection.

There are many agencies offering support to those bereaved by suicide and these are listed in the Appendix.

## Death by Murder

*"Our daughter was beautiful, she was an angel. The thought of someone violating her, of her suffering, of not being able to get help, of us not protecting her crucifies us every minute of every day. No-one can ever know how it tortures us and how it has*

*destroyed our lives. My husband and I have
separated, he couldn't live with it. He says that it's
the guilt; he feels guilty because he thinks we should
have saved her. I feel dead, completely dead. I don't
want to live but I fight it because if I give in then
her murderer has won."*

*"He will come out of prison one day but we will be
in prison forever. She is gone forever. Her children
will never know her. People offer words, they try to
offer hope, they think they understand but no-one
can know this unless they have lived through it. This
is hell!"*

*"My husband was attacked by a gang, he was
kicked so violently that it caused him trauma and
he died. They write about it in newspapers.
Everyone knows, and when they meet me they say
they are sorry but no-one can offer me anything
that can come near to stopping this pain in me. I
have nightmares about his death and I sometimes
think I might know his killers and fear for my
safety. I can't begin to tell you how this has changed
me: I am destroyed."*

When a loved one is murdered the impact this has on
those who cared about them is different from that
created by any other cause of death. The death of a
loved one at the hand of another, violently, can cause
deep and ongoing trauma for the families. Those
bereaved by murder are tortured by the revelations of
how their loved one died, and how they may have
suffered. Added media attention and publicity means
that they are exposed to and immersed in public

attention, often insensitively. Many of us will recall observing the shocked families of murder victims appealing for help on television and reading their stories in newspapers.

At that time the shocked family is carried along by the police, press and public and the whole business of attention. They lose their own identity and are now identified by what they have been through. The emphasis is on 'how well' they are coping or 'how brave' the family are. They may be treated as heroes, the 'brave and courageous family of murder victim X'. They are interviewed on TV and their vulnerability is exploited by those keen to produce a good media story, thus creating an unspoken, added pressure on them to remain dignified.

The initial attention may give them a sense that their grief has been acknowledged, the publicity and attention they receive showing them that people care but, as time passes and the attention fades, they are left to face the reality of bereavement by murder and they can feel deserted and forgotten.

*"At first we didn't feel so alone, letters arrived daily – too many to read some days – but it seemed that so many people were out there, shocked by our son's murder, and wanting to let us know they cared. After the trial and the newspaper reports and a few occasional public statements, we were finally alone and it was then that our hell began. It felt unbelievable that our son wasn't coming home. I had kept every article, videoed every interview on TV and we (my husband and I) went over and over it all. No matter how many times we did, it didn't make sense. It felt unreal, inconceivable. The worst*

*was thinking about the pain he endured. We weren't
there for him."*

There are many emotions experienced by the family of a
murder victim: pity or forgiveness perhaps, but more
likely rage, anger and thoughts of revenge. Revenge may
be thought about or planned, but not spoken of. It is
usual for all whose loved one died at the hands of
another to feel vengeful at some time or other. These
feelings can be the cause of added anxieties within
families, and need to be heard, rationalised and
explored.

*"My wife says that feeling the way I feel is eating
away at who I am, who I was. I will never be the
same again. This person murdered my son and I
want to see him. I want to seek him out. I will wait
for him to be released and I will find him. That is
my purpose in life."*

*"I felt bitter, twisted with hatred for seven years
after my husband died. I planned how I would hurt
his killer, I fantasised about it and I was consumed
by it. It changed me and then I realised that he was
killing me too and everything our family meant. I
had to let go of my rage to survive it, though I will
never forgive him."*

*"I cling to religion. I hope there is a God and that
he will punish this person – it's all I have."*

The families and friends of murder victims may experience a deep sense of helplessness and self-torture, reliv-
ing in their imagination the last moments of their

loved ones, frustrated by their inability to protect and defend the victim from this evil deed. Their eventual realisation that, no matter what punishment the killer may receive, it will not heal their grief or compensate them for their loss of their loved one, becomes a positive step in their journey towards acceptance.

There seems little to offer the parents of a murdered child, the children of a murdered parent or the bereaved partners other than the facility for them openly and unashamedly to share their thoughts and feelings without having to consider the sensibilities of the listener. Their anguish needs to be acknowledged and accepted. We have to try and avoid the temptation to try to fix or compensate what, in reality, we cannot. They need to feel that they can express their rage openly at another human being taking away the life of someone they loved, and to work through all aspects and emotions that may eventually lead to acceptance.

# 6

# 'DEAR ALEX . . .'

Since focusing all my energies on bereavement, I have through various Internet websites become an 'online' grief/bereavement counsellor, mentor and agony aunt. I work voluntarily and receive emails daily from people all over the world who have lost a beloved and cherished person, someone very dear to them, and who seek reassurance, the opportunity to share their intimate feelings and to tell their story and, most importantly of all, to feel acknowledged.

I would like to thank each and every individual who has generously given me their permission to use the following letters. Many of these people have been corresponding with me for a time and still receive my on-going support.

Thank you.

All the letters I receive are as individual as the people who write them, but many of them address similar concerns or feelings, so I have grouped them together under the most commonly expressed views for the reader's ease of reference.

## Waiting to Die
This might sound odd to anyone who has not experienced a close bereavement, but a lot of bereaved people

use this expression. Many grieving people feel this way, but are unable to express it openly and this can leave them with a sense of isolation and thinking that they are going crazy and that perhaps they are the only people, ever, to think this way.

*"I think, one day further from my child being alive, but one day nearer to being with him."*

Another person said:

*"Before this happened, I used to think, 'What if they told me I had a terminal illness, only a short while to live?' I'd be devastated. I'd fight it. But since her death, in some ways I would be glad – it would mean release from this pain, a way out."*

These feelings and thoughts are, as I have discovered, usual and often unspoken. People who have not been through this experience might be unable to comprehend or be horrified that such words can be said and be thought acceptable, but 'waiting to die', as an escape from pain and from the life that has changed so much and is no longer recognisable as your own, does not mean you are going to take your own life. The two are very different. Comments such as, "I cannot live without him/her" or "I feel my life is finished" are descriptions, communications of feelings that are so deep, so intensely painful, that living on can seem intolerable.

Sometimes the bereaved person can take risks, doing things that before may have caused them deep anxiety or fear.

*"I used to fear flying but now I just think — what
the hell. In fact, if something happens, I will not
have to endure this agony."*

They may feel as if the joy and colour in life has been
stripped from it, but alongside this the bereaved survive.
Waiting to die.

*Dear Alex*
*    You know, I never thought anyone else had these
feelings but me. I used to tell my husband after our
child died of leukaemia that I was ready to die too.
Before her death I was always afraid of dying, but
since she has gone I am ready, sometimes I just
need to be near her. I miss her so much that I am
ready . . . not fearful. Does that make sense? I don't
know. I would never take my life. I wouldn't do that.
It's just how I feel.*
*    From Bess*

*Dear Alex*
*    I feel just like this. I am facing the prospect of
having cancer and, yes, it scares me, but somehow it
is different now that my son died. The problem I
have most is the hurt and agony the ones around me
feel. I came in from work yesterday to find my wife
sobbing. She is so fearful of what might happen if I
die. I could only tell her that I am not going to —
she won't get rid of me that easily. If she didn't hurt
so much, if I could take away her pain, it wouldn't
be so hard.*
*    From M*

*Dear Alex*

*It just seems peaceful, kind of 'I don't care if death comes', I don't fear it any longer. My family would never understand it, this feeling I have. I have this feeling from suffering loss. It so helps to know that others think and feel this way, that I'm not crazy, that it's OK. For the most part I think that society judges it unacceptable as self-pity.*

*Thanks for reading.*

*KK*

*Dear Alex*

*The loss we experience as parents affects us in many ways I could never have imagined or thought possible. After losing my daughter Kristina I look at it totally differently. She was 20 when she died, living without her is hell. There is no place to go but to be with her, and some days I think sooner rather than later. I have no fear of death – some days it's just not soon enough. No, I'm not crazy, I just miss her.*

*From Krissy's mom*

*Dear Alex*

*I thought I was alone until I read that others feel as I do. My 18-year-old committed suicide two years ago. I often feel I just want to die. Sometimes I think that my husband and remaining children would get over it. Reality comes back to roost though and I would never hurt my family, put them through that. I just keep going, one day after another.*

*I feel no joy, no happiness. I am empty. I am on anti-depressants and I feel I want to cry most of the*

*time. I cannot tell you how thrilled I am to think
this is normal. I thought no-one thought like me –
had these thoughts. Many times individuals have
tried to comfort me and tell me that I will be with
my son for eternity. I reply that eternity is until the
day I can hold him in my arms again, that is
eternity.*

*Thank you.*
*From C*

## Hope

Has this really happened? Is there any hope?

People who have not experienced a close bereavement
may not understand this kind of hope. How can there
be hope when a loved one has died? However, this
feeling of hope is a very common feeling experienced by
many who have been bereaved. People often tell me that
during the first few months of bereavement, they have a
sense of hope: hope that their loved one will return to
them, that what has happened is not real, that they are
caught up in some nightmarish situation, that it is all a
mistake and will soon return to how it was before, back
to normal.

Sometimes the bereaved try to re-enact an event, or
repeat behaviour, or may try to keep things the same. If
no changes are made, time may stand still and they may
somehow find a way back to how things were, recover
the past and their loved one.

These feelings of hope can be comforting and can form
part of the grieving process and journey towards acceptance. In between these feelings there may be other more
easily talked about feelings of anger, guilt and despair
coupled with moments of joy. This confusing and diverse
rollercoaster of feelings, thoughts and emotions is an

exhausting time for the bereaved.

The sense of hope does not grow from disbelief, although this may seem the case to an observer. It is the desire for the situation to be unreal, the mind's battle towards the eventual acceptance of the unacceptable. This is the language of grief at its very core of being – "I know my child is dead but I hope . . ."

*Dear Alex*

*Well, I know she is gone. I know it. But for some reason, inside, I am programmed to wait for her before I can begin preparing for Christmas. Does it sound crazy? Am I absolutely bonkers? I know she isn't coming; she's never coming again – I went and decorated her grave for Pete's sake! In a few moments of sanity I even bought some presents for out of town people I need to send to, but I never mailed them. They just sit here on December 18th unmailed. My baking ingredients are purchased and I cannot bake. I turn on the oven a few times daily, like today, but nothing goes in it.*

*Why can't I stop this feeling that she will come, walk in the door any minute, signal the beginning of Christmas? Hey, any second now she'll be here or call, then I can start.*

*From Marilyn*

*Dear Alex*

*I am very concerned about my friend. Her daughter died six months ago, but my Mum told me that she still waits for her to come. Sometimes she sits on the sofa and waits. She hopes to hear her daughter's familiar rat-tat on the door and her voice as she arrives. It is difficult to talk to her. She says she knows Deidre is dead, but she hopes.*

*Please, if you can explain this, if I can understand what she is feeling, I might be able to help her a little.*

*Thank you.*

*Julia*


*Dear Alex*

*My husband died almost a year ago but I keep on getting this weird feeling, it's like, hope, but I know there isn't any.*

*When our children are out or in bed and I'm on my own I listen for his car on the drive. I wait for him to come. I know he isn't coming, I know he is deceased.*

*I am not afraid of what I feel, more concerned that I'm going mad. If you can offer any advice or information, I'd be so grateful.*

*Thank you.*

*Alice*


*Dear Alex*

*I am a bereaved father. My only son Joey died just before Christmas. I don't think there is a moment when I am not thinking about him but the feeling of anticipation at times is huge. I frequently anticipate seeing him, hearing him outside and his familiar voice. I'm hoping but I know there isn't any hope. I can't talk about this to anyone, I'd think they'd think I was crazy. Hope you can help me.*

*Thanks.*

*Tom*

## Dreams and Nightmares

We all dream, but to the bereaved the quiet hours of the night are often the times when their innermost thoughts, fears and hopes about their deceased loved ones materialise in their dreams. It is usual and some bereaved people may find comfort in what they perceive to be further contact with their deceased loved one whereas others can be caused additional distress as they relive in their dreams parts of their life they would rather put behind them. The mind can play tricks when people are in emotional turmoil and incidents which occur in dreams can take on a huge significance to a bereaved person.

*Dear Alex*

*In the first few days/weeks after my son died I kept having the same nightmare. It was as things happened on that day but with some changes. It starts out with that feeling – that I have to go and check on Kyle NOW, but when I get up and start to walk down the hall to his room, which is only about 15 feet, the hall gets longer and longer. So I start to run and, after what seems like forever, I get to his room, but in the dream I don't get to start CPR. It ends with me standing in the doorway and screaming his name.*

*I also dream about showing up at my parents' house unexpectedly. My parents and sister are there. I walk into the house without knocking, just as I always do and Kyle is standing there. He's alive, but, when he turns and sees me, he runs and hides from me. I am searching all over for him but no-one will tell me where he has hidden. I am begging my parents to tell me where he is, asking*

them how this could happen and why they didn't tell
me.

Finally, they tell me he hasn't really died; he just
didn't want to see me again, that he faked hanging
himself and everyone lied about his death because
he hated me. It ends with me sobbing and begging
him and everyone else to understand that I loved
him and me telling him that he didn't have to clean
his room, that I will do it, if he'll just please forgive
me and let me hug him, but everyone ignores me. I
wake up sobbing.

From Kyle's Mum

My reply to Kyle's Mum:

Dear Kyle's Mum

You sound like you loved your son, Kyle, very
much but his tragic death has left you with so much
self-blame.

You sound like every mum I have ever met,
including myself. Telling a child to do things over
and over, getting irritated when he doesn't do it is
usual parent/child stuff.

It sounds as if Kyle chose to do this in a moment
of despair. I doubt he planned it through or did it
having really considered the consequences. So often
children feel a certain way and act on it and in
Kyle's circumstances the consequences were beyond
your reach, prevention or protection.

This is so very tragic and traumatic and I
understand the torment you feel, the torture of
self-blame you are going through. Your dream is so
full of anguish, pain and loss, as is your belief and
thoughts that it is your fault, that he hated, blamed

*and rejected you. It also sounds as though you feel
judged by others. The death of your baby without
your being able to make it up with him has left you
searching emotionally, mentally and physically for
answers. Clearly you loved your son very much and
the self-blame for his death leads you to punish
yourself and deny your good mothering and believe
you were a bad mother.*

*I wonder if you are able to think back to when
Kyle was alive, think back to another time when you
asked him to complete a chore, a time when he had
also refused and you argued. Now, think what
happened after that, after you had reinforced your
wish and he had done what you had asked. You
probably made up. Think about the times you've
cuddled him, kissed him, told him you loved him,
done things for him and had fun. When you recall
those times you know he knew you loved him.*

*It sounds as though he did this without proper
thought of consequences, in a pique of anger,
sadness or frustration and I doubt that it was
planned. When people/children act on impulse they
can make mistakes that may be fatal.*

*I hope you can begin to give yourself permission
to accept that you are not to blame and allow
yourself to grieve for your son.*

*Alex*


*Dear Alex*

*I have been having this dream on and off since
my husband died six months ago. Please can you
help me make sense of it. It is very distressing.*

*I dream that I am going to meet him. I am very
excited. It feels like it is over, he isn't dead after all*

*and I'm going to tell him how awful it has been
without him. I go into this room and he is standing
with his back to me. I go towards him but he doesn't
respond. Then he opens a door and goes through
and the door closes. I wake up in a real state and I
am usually calling out to him and asking him not to
go.*

    *Helen*

My reply to Helen was:

*Dear Helen*

    *Your dream really sounds distressing, a reflection
of how you feel. Your husband has died and you
long for it not to be true. You cannot find him and
when you think you have he doesn't respond, leaves
and is gone and you awake distressed.*

    *These dreams are quite usual. Often people tell
me that they dream about their loved one in a crowd
or across the street but being restricted from getting
there or the person moves away. The deep anguish
of loss, the desire to make things better or how they
were, the hope that it isn't true create the dream of
searching and finding.*

    *The reality of all that has happened, the truth,
creates a sense of loss. It sounds to me as though
you are fighting with the acceptance of all that has
happened. You desire it not to be true but you know
it is true.*

    *Alex*

**Anguish and Shock**

*Dear Alex*

*Today I am experiencing all of this. Today I could lie on the floor of concrete and push my face as deep into it as I could. Most days I do OK but we all know we will never experience the joy of having a perfect day again.*

*After six years of living without the awesome smile of my Elizabeth I still experience the same pain as I did in the beginning, I just hide it better after so many years of practice. Those words about wanting everyone who passes us to know hit me so hard, how sad to have a wish like this.*

*As hard as I try, I cannot get through the day without tears. Thank you for writing this; it is always a comfort to know that others understand.*

*Julie*

*Dear Alex*

*When they told me he had died, my world began to shake, the room was spinning. I can't remember it all but I know I knelt on the floor with my arms over the chair. I have this pain across my chest like being crucified, my heart ripped out. I begged them to say it was a mistake.*

*There were moments when I felt in control, almost stony, absent feelings and I could put words together and make arrangements, even supporting others. People said I was doing well, like praise. I felt like I should be doing more. I went out at night looking but I can't say what for. I blame myself, I let him down, I should have been there, I failed. I need to be strong but I don't know how.*

*Sometimes I thought about dying, escaping the pain. I won't do it though because I can't put the family through any more.*

*Sometimes it just hits me, he really is dead. Sometimes I hold it in, afraid that if I let it out, start to cry, I'll never stop.*

*I don't know how life will be now. I think about the years ahead. I envy the elderly because for them life will soon be over. I know nothing any more, just existing.*

*Thanks for reading.*
*Hanna*

*Dear Alex*
*I read Hanna's letter. A lot of this is exactly how I felt the day I was told. Reading this lets me know I'm not entirely alone as it feels. Thank you.*
*Julian*

## Worries about Burials and Cremation

*Dear Alex*
*My daughter died 18 months ago and we decided to have her buried close to my parents, her grandparents, who died ten years and eight years ago. At first I gained a sense of comfort from knowing that she was near my parents and if ever I thought about her grave and the dark or cold I would think about how much my parents loved her and the fact that they were nearby helped. Lately though I have felt more concerned about my daughter. I cannot stop thinking about her beautiful body, her lovely smile, and all that may be going on beneath the soil. I'm thinking about the destruction*

*of her, the decomposition and it is torturous. I know this sounds silly but it's bad enough to bear that she is dead without thinking about further damage. Please tell me if these thoughts are normal.*

*Thank you.*

*Stevie*

My reply:

*Dear Stevie*

*In my experience, yes, many of these thoughts are usual/normal. So often these thoughts and feelings are experienced in isolation as the fear of disclosing thoughts like these is that others may be horrified, may not understand and may be concerned for the well-being of the bereaved.*

*It is as you say hard and torturous enough to endure the pain and grief for the death of your beautiful child without thinking about her grave and ongoing decomposition.*

*These are very real and painful thoughts and the reality is that over time her remains will decompose. It is not at all silly and I can only offer my reassurance that you are not alone. Talking these thoughts through will help you to come towards some level of manageability and acceptance. If you are unable to find someone trusted with whom to share, please do write to me again.*

*Alex*

*Dear Alex*

*Thank you for offering your support to bereaved folk like me. I have read a lot of your words and it is comforting to know that others in this world feel and think some of the stuff I do.*

*I am writing to you because I don't want to ask
anyone who knows me and I can't dare tell my
family what's in my head. My husband died six
months ago and ever since we buried him I have felt
distraught, not only about his death but because he
is buried. I can't seem to get him out of my head
down in the deep dark earth and I think about him
and I feel so consumed by this need to get him out.
I think I'm going crazy. I have tried to stop but I
just can't. Please tell me if others have these
thoughts.*
*Anon*

My reply:
*Yes, others do have these thoughts. Sometimes
there are concerns about the weather, about cold or
rain, and on several occasions people have told me
that they have felt compelled to clear snow from
their loved one's grave or had thoughts about the
grave being wet. The sense of transferred
claustrophobia . . . Fantasising about the deceased
being trapped below ground or being afraid is also
not unusual. The hardest part of acceptance is the
reality that he is dead, that in being dead he is not
experiencing these elements that are disturbing you
and that by retrieving his remains you cannot bring
back his life. I wonder if this is more about the need
to have him back, the deep loss and missing his
presence?*

*I feel you would certainly benefit from good
professional support and urge you to seek this, as
within a trusted relationship the opportunity to
explore these feelings at greater depth will be
beneficial.*

*Dear Alex*

*I have tried to find some answers myself but it seems there is a lot of secrecy about death and when I have attempted to talk about it friends and family seem horrified and try to distract me by changing the subject. I'd like to know what happens to a body when it is cremated. My husband was cremated and I have just received his ashes, I don't think there are enough. Also how can I be sure they are his? I have heard a lot of stories about cremations. Please help. Any answers to my questions will be appreciated.*

*Angela*

My reply:

*Dear Angela*

*I can only speak from my own experience but I will try to answer your questions.*

*It may be possible to visit the crematorium (some encourage visitors to look around and are available to answer questions; some offer open days).*

*The process of cremation is the disposal of human remains by burning at a very high temperature. Nothing is removed from the coffin or casket prior to cremation and the dressings provided on the coffin such as handles, etc, are all of disposable material. Items such as metal photo frames or jewellery will be returned to the family.*

*Once the cremation process is completed, any remaining ash and bone are removed and scanned for metal content. They are then placed into a machine that grinds them to fine dust. Finally the dust/ashes are transferred to either a plastic bag or an urn.*

*Bodies are never cremated with other bodies and the ashes you receive will be only of one person. Yes, it does seem impossible that a whole person can be reduced to such a small amount of powder and you are not alone in thinking these thoughts but I offer my confirmation that this is how it is.*
*    Alex*

*Dear Alex*
*    My wife died a year ago and is buried. I often think about her beneath the ground and I can't get the thoughts out of my head once they start. Can you please tell me how long it takes for a body to decompose completely? I don't know why I am in need of this information. Am I being morbid and do others feel this way?*
*    David*

My reply:
*Dear David*
*    Decomposure begins soon after death and progresses until there is only solid matter such as bone left which in certain conditions and with the passage of time may also reduce.*
*    If the body has been embalmed and, depending on the degree of embalming that has taken place, decomposure may take longer. Ground conditions also impact the speed at which decomposure progresses. If the ground is wetter, the decomposure is likely to be quicker. I have been told that in many cases by around 18 months the body will have mostly decomposed.*
*    In answer to your question – No, you are not alone in having these thoughts. Although some may*

*feel that it is morbid, I believe it is quite usual to want to know these things. Being able to ask such questions and to receive the appropriate information can be a positive move towards managing your grief.*
   *Alex*

*Dear Alex*
   *My family are arguing about my daughter's ashes (she died of illness and was cremated a year ago). My ex -, her mother, wants to place her ashes in a local cemetery but I would like to scatter them in a park where we spent many happy hours together. Someone has suggested we split them. Is this an acceptable thing to do? I mentioned it to a friend and she was horrified but frankly my ex-wife and I feel OK with it. Your thoughts on this matter would be greatly appreciated.*
   *Tony*

My reply:
   *Dear Tony*
   *I believe that whatever you as individuals feel is right for you is the right thing to do. No, it isn't at all unusual for families to 'split' or share the ashes of their loved one particularly where families may be separated. It may be difficult for those who are not as closely involved or who have never experienced a death to understand fully how it feels or the needs of the bereaved. It is important that you do whatever gives you comfort. It sounds like you had a very special relationship with your daughter and leaving something of her at your special place sounds fine.*
   *Alex*

# APPENDIX

**The Samaritans**
PO Box 9090, Stirling, FK8 2SA
Tel: 08457 90 90 90 (24 hours, every day)
www.samaritans.org

**Cruse Bereavement Care**
Cruse House, 126 Sheen Road, Richmond, Surrey,
TW9 1UR
Tel: 0870 167 1677
www.crusebereavementcare.org.uk
Email: helpline@crusebereavementcare.org.uk

**The Compassionate Friends**
53 North Street, Bristol, BS3 1EN
Tel: 0117 966 5202
Helpline: 08451 23 23 04 (10 am to 4 pm; 6.30 pm to
10.30 pm every day)
www.tcf.org.uk

**The Foundation for the Study of Infant Deaths**
Artillery House, 11–19 Artillery Row, London, SW1P 1RT
Helpline: 0870 787 0554
www.sids.org.uk/fsid
Email: fsid@sids.org.uk

**The National Association of Widows**
National Office, 48 Queens Road, Coventry, CV1 3EH
Tel: 024 7663 4848
www.widows.uk.net

**Support after Murder and Manslaughter**
Cranmer House, 39 Brixton Road, London, SW9 6DZ
Tel: 020 7735 3838
www.samm.org.uk

**Road Peace**
(support and information for those bereaved by road
crash)
PO Box 2579, London, NW10 3PW
Tel: 020 8838 5102
www.roadpeace.org
Email: info@roadpeace.org

**National Aids Foundation**
New City Cloisters, 196 Old Street, London, EC1V 9FR
Tel: 020 7814 6767
www.nat.org.uk
Email: info@nat.org.uk

**BACUP**
(cancer support and information)
Freephone Helpline: 0808 800 1234
www.cancerbacup.org.uk

**Victim Support**
UK National Office, Cranmer House, 39 Brixton Road,
London, SW9 6DZ
Tel: 020 7735 9166
www.victimsupport.org.uk